NATIONAL BANKRUPTCY

Why The Middle Class Is Doomed

By James R Cook

TABLE OF CONTENTS

INTRODUCTION

Nobody knows the future. We can only make intelligent guesses. Some people are optimistic. Others like this writer have a gloomy prognosis. Over the past 15 years our warnings have been surprisingly accurate. In January 2000 just weeks before the Nasdaq bubble burst we wrote, "For those who think the stock market will never crash, here are 20 powerful reasons." In 2002 we wrote about the housing boom, "Years of inflationary money and credit creation have fostered unmanageable levels of debt and spending. Now the debt is beginning to strangle us. An agonizing liquidation will sweep homeowners and mortgage lenders away on a tidal wave of foreclosures."

Now we are warning about government spending and borrowing excesses that put us at the mercy of circumstances we can't control. Foreign bond holders have leverage over us like never before; our central bank may have to create so much new money that inflation runs away. The dollar can fall precipitously in foreign exchange markets. All these negative factors are intertwined and one can set off the other. Suffice to say that we face a major crisis ahead.

We don't believe government spending will be cut. There are thousands of government spending programs. Try to reduce one and there is a public uproar. Cuts will come but they will be forced on us by the markets. Runaway government spending will end when the markets push us into bankruptcy.

This day of reckoning (or month or year) appears to be fast approaching. The proposed cures for our dire predicament are more of the same bad economic choices that got us into trouble in the first place. Basically the monetary authorities have one overriding policy: print up a bunch of new money. Inflating is the oldest fallacy. It places us in grave financial peril. Nothing will turn the politicians and the central bank around. They will follow their Keynesian dogma to the bitter end. This book is about the causes and consequences of our coming downfall.

CHAPTER ONE
ONE HELLISH PREDICAMENT

*"The only way to effectively secure the common good is for government to
remain small."*
— Joel Miller

*"Our nation is in deep trouble – morally, economically, and politically. Practi-
cally everything in which the federal government has embroiled itself for the
last several decades is in crisis – education, Social Security, Medicare, Medicaid, inflation and the dollar, welfare, government spending, the drug war, and,
of course, foreign policy."*
— Jacob G. Hornberger

Nothing defines a country like the soundness of its money. No nation can
afford to have its money dramatically lose purchasing power. That country
will be punished in foreign exchange markets and its global influence will
diminish. If a nation covers its overspending by printing money (monetizing
its debt) the currency of that country will depreciate. If this process of paying bills with newly created money continues, as it has in the United States, it
ensures dollar devaluation. This constant money and credit expansion to pay
for runaway spending will inevitably destroy the value of the dollar. Make no
mistake about it, the dollar can be rendered worthless.

Every financial decision a person makes should keep this thought in mind. If
the government persists in covering its debt with newly created purchasing
media the dollar will fail. Dollars are like anything else, if there's an over-sup-
ply the value falls. A glut cheapens the value of an item. Unfortunately for the
U.S., falling tax revenues and excessive spending have created a gargantuan
deficit that must be covered by government borrowing or money printing. You
can only borrow so much and then you must create new dollars out of thin
air. That's happening now.

Washington, Wall Street and the foolish Keynesians of the New York Times
insist that inflation (dollar depreciation) is not a problem. They've been saying these things for decades. The best way to judge their argument is to look
backwards. When I started in business a loaf of bread was a quarter. There are
a million examples like that. What we've been told about low inflation is as
truthful as what Bernie Madoff told his investors.

These modern Keynesians argue for greater government spending (bigger deficits) and care little of the consequences. John Maynard Keynes would never condone the excessive government spending of today. Keynes viewed inflating as a threat and expected any excessive purchasing media to be withdrawn in good economic times. Pumping out money has become the central bank's answer to recession but taking it back has gone the way of the passenger pigeon.

Here's the rub, the nation's expenditures are totally out of control and a balanced budget may be impossible. One side blames military spending and the other blames social spending. It's the latter that threatens to break the bank because the voters won't sanction cuts. Government employees, unions, subsidized citizens and politicians on the left insist on massive social spending. It's impossible to cut these growing programs because so many people have come to rely on them. There's a certain amount of heartlessness in repealing them. Unfortunately, they carry the seeds of their own undoing. Social Security, Medicare, Medicaid, subsidized housing, food stamps, welfare *ad infinitum* are like an aneurism. The bigger it gets the greater threat it is to the host, until it finally bursts and kills the patient.

An article in our local newspaper chronicled the work of two young ladies who recently graduated from law school. They were busily enrolling homeless men for Social Security disability payments so that these alcoholics and addicts could get a monthly check (in addition to whatever other subsidies they got). What once was a retirement plan has morphed into a massive social welfare scheme with millions of recipients who contributed nothing. I don't need to tell you about escalating costs in Medicare and Medicaid. These are financial backbreakers that simply cannot be funded out of government revenues. Consequently the currency must be inflated until its value becomes suspect.

Those who claim inflation is not a problem never mention that the sound dollar of yesterday is now worth $.02 in current purchasing power. Nor do they seem to realize that price inflation can accelerate for reasons other than high consumer demand, rising wages and a business boom. Inflation can soar upward from a falling dollar. Imports and commodity prices will rise if the dollar drops in international markets. A sinking dollar means higher prices for natural resources, food and oil.

We are in between a rock and a hard place. The government insists on breaking the bank with its spending. Our runaway social costs can't be stopped without blood in the streets. A tax hike will harm the economy. You could double taxes and we'd still be deep in the red. Continued money printing (quantitative easing) will ruin the dollar.

We can't be certain about coming events but it's easy to conclude that Washington Keynesians will make poor choices. The nation's fate is tied to the dollar. This is the worst economic mess in history. All you can do is look out for your financial well-being, practice charity and support those who want to lead the nation out of this terrible predicament.

CHAPTER TWO
HANGING TOGETHER

"All the fiery rhetoric of the founders was directed at a 'tyrant' who taxed his subjects at a rate of about three percent. Today, we in the 'land of the free' are taxed at about 50 percent when you add federal, state, and local taxes. What kind of government would do this?"
– Doug Newman

"What both the left and the right overlook is our Founders' wisdom about the limits and dangers of government."
– Edward H. Crane

"A limited government is a contradiction in terms."
– Robert LeFevre

How do we know our political views are correct? On the left, liberals are certain of their intellectual superiority. This snobbery allows them to scorn anyone with differing views. Among conservatives, the neo-cons aim to make government bigger and more intrusive. On what basis can we build a powerful argument against those on the left or right who want to force their agenda down our throats?

Our founding fathers are a good place to start. When Benjamin Franklin stated, "It would be thought a hard government that should tax its people one tenth part," he never dreamed the American people would hold still for today's taxes of 50%. Those of us who oppose higher taxes and advocate limited government are in much better company than the liberals and neo-cons who would find no favor with our founders.

Thomas Jefferson put it this way: "A wise and frugal government, which shall leave men free to regulate their own pursuits of industry and improvement, and shall not take from the mouth of labor the bread it has earned – this is the sum of good government." What we have today then is the sum of bad government. Jefferson warned about the eventual outcome of income transfers. "The democracy will cease to exist when you take away from those who are willing to work and give to those who would not." Jefferson went on to say, "I predict future happiness for Americans if they can prevent the government from wasting the labors of the people under the pretense of taking care of them."

It hasn't worked out that way. Socialist schemes administered by government squander our tax dollars and social costs are running away. You can have socialism, but you can't have prosperity. As the great Austrian social economist Ludwig von Mises instructed, "Socialism [modern liberalism] is not in the least what it pretends to be. It is not the pioneer of a better and finer world, but the spoiler of what thousands of years of civilization have created. It does not build; it destroys. For destruction is the essence of it. It produces nothing, it only consumes what the social order based on private ownership of the means of production has created."

Mises further stated, "A man who chooses between drinking a glass of milk and a glass of a solution of potassium cyanide does not choose between two beverages; he chooses between life and death. A society that chooses between capitalism and socialism does not choose between two social systems; it chooses between social cooperation and the disintegration of society. Socialism is not an alternative to capitalism; it is an alternative to any system under which men can live as human beings."

We are in the early stages of the disintegration of our society. Multiculturalism, inflation, high taxes and a huge, growing underclass will see to that. Disparaging the free market is another sign of backwardness and coming chaos. Envy; hatred of the producers, anti-business propaganda, punishment of the rich; expropriation of wealth; the politics of class warfare: all are in vogue. Worst of all, the government is destroying the dollar. Through its big spending, social schemes and foreign adventures, it must inflate to stay afloat. The flaw in paper money is that it can be created at will by politicians and bureaucrats to meet any contingency. At some point hyperinflation is inevitable. That will tear the social fabric further as the nimble become richer and the masses become poorer.

Each of us carries a responsibility to preserve our freedom and the greatness of our nation. We must gain enough understanding of the threat from within - the reigning dogma of the left. We must become beacons of economic education and influence in checking the inroads of socialism. "It's one mind at a time," said my mentor, the late Bernard Daley. He saw the writing on the walls years ago and vigorously warned about the inroads of socialism and the destruction it would make inevitable.

The socialist leader, Norman Thomas, once said, "The American people will never knowingly adopt socialism, but under the name of liberalism, they will adopt every fragment of the socialist program until one day America will be a socialist nation without ever knowing how it happened." Fear for your country if that proves to be true.

The patriots who drafted the Declaration of Independence risked all. One tragic reversal and Washington, Jefferson, Franklin and the others would have quickly been hung from a tree and you would never have heard of them. The guidance they provided for controlling government has been rejected by the free spending pols of today. We have ignored the guidance of our founders and we will pay a price. Hopefully, the excruciating setbacks we suffer will make us harken once again to their wisdom.

CHAPTER THREE
THE ECONOMIST

"Socialist practices are now so ingrained in our thinking, so customary, so much a part of our mores, that we take them for granted." – Leonard Read

"The truly free market is the worker's best friend." – Sheldon Richman

Ludwig von Mises (1881-1973) (pronounced Meesez) was born in the Austro-Hungarian empire. Hard money advocates and free market economists consider him to be the greatest economic thinker in history. He believed in limited government, the gold standard, sound money, capitalism and personal freedom. If you have never heard of him, it's time you learned more. Mises attended the University of Vienna during the high tide of the "Austrian School" of economics. His accomplishments are prodigious. In 1920, he showed that socialism and planning must fail because of the lack of market pricing. Mises' insightful checkmate to collectivism was widely acknowledged when communism collapsed seventy years later.

Among other things, Mises was able to show that inflation was no more than taxation and redistribution of wealth; that prices will most often fall without government induced money injections; that increases in the money supply, e.g. a sudden doubling of everyone's money holding benefits society not an iota and in fact only dilutes purchasing power; that only growth in the factors of production, land, labor, plant and equipment will increase production and standards of living.

In a brilliant and important theoretical accomplishment Mises answered a problem most economists thought unanswerable. How can we explain that the price of money is influenced by demand if to have demand it must first have a price? He traced the origin of money back in time to a useful barter commodity (e.g. silver and gold).

The dramatic implication was that money could only originate on the free market out of demand. Government, despite any attempts to the contrary, could not originate money. Money is not arbitrary pieces of paper but must originate as a useful and valuable commodity. Mises also pointed out how central banking acts as an accomplice to government money expansion. And he began to explain his great business cycle theory. Recognizing that the market economy could not generate by itself a series of booms and busts he fixed the blame on an outside factor – the habitual expansion of money and credit.

He argued that a credit-induced boom must eventually "lead to a crack-up boom." He wrote, "The boom can last only as long as the credit expansion progresses at an ever-accelerated pace. The boom comes to an end as soon as additional quantities of fiduciary media are no longer thrown upon the loan market. But it could not last forever even if inflation and credit expansion were to go on endlessly. It would then encounter the barriers which prevent the boundless expansion of circulation credit. It would lead to the crack-up boom and the breakdown of the whole monetary system."

He warned, "The credit expansion boom is built on the sands of banknotes and deposits. It must collapse." He stated, "If the credit expansion is not stopped in time, the boom turns into the crackup boom; the flight into real values begins, and the whole monetary system founders. Continuous inflation (credit expansion) must finally end in the crack-up boom and the complete break-down of the currency system."

Mises further claimed, "Expansion (of credit) squanders scarce factors of production by malinvestment and overconsumption." Malinvestment means building shopping centers rather than factories. Overconsumption means a borrowing and spending boom by consumers that depletes savings and reduces capital investment.

Mises was aware that a credit excess could spill over into stock and bond speculation. But even he would be surprised at today's unprecedented level of credit-induced speculation. He would be depressed by the astonishing levels of public and private debt, government borrowing, central bank market interventions, trade deficits, non-bank credit growth, money velocity, illiquidity, overconsumption and foreign indebtedness. Can these phenomena persist?

Absolutely not says Mises. "Credit expansion is not a nostrum to make people happy. The boom it engenders must inevitably lead to a debacle and unhappiness." He warned, "Accidental, institutional, and psychological circumstances generally turn the outbreak of the crisis into a panic. The description of these awful events can be left to the historians. It is not... (our task)... to depict in detail the calamities of panicky days and weeks and to dwell upon their sometimes grotesque aspects."

"The final outcome of the credit expansion is general impoverishment. Some people may have increased their wealth; they did not let their reasoning be obfuscated by the mass hysteria, and took advantage in time of the opportunities offered by the mobility of the individual investor... but the immense majority must foot the bill for the malinvestments and the overconsumption of the boom episode."

Austrian economics rests on the foundation of readily observable human actions. Beings have goals, they set out to attain them; they have individual preferences; and they act within the framework of time. Each person and his or her actions are different and unique. The very nature of human behavior defies economic codification.

Mises points out that there are not quantitative constants in human behavior. In his greatest book, "Human Action," he developed a rational economic science based on this human factor. At the same time he tweaked the nose of today's highly popular mathematical economics, statistical economics and econometrics. This posturing and economic forecasting he dismissed as little more than poppycock.

In the early thirties, Austrian school economics was on the verge of carrying the day. But in England, the publication of John Maynard Keynes', *General Theory of Employment, Interest and Money*, provided the rationalizations necessary for politicians and government to spend and inflate endlessly. Until that moment virtually the entire body and history of economic thought stood against such theories. But, Keynes' theories fit hand in glove with the mentality of intervention and statism. It rationalized politicians, economists and governments jumping in bed together to expand their power and influence.

Not that Mises was rebutted or that anyone overturned his conclusions – he was simply ignored. How many Americans have ever heard of Ludwig von Mises? How many businessmen know that he placed the girders and underpinnings under free enterprise that cement that system to reason? How many know that he won the moral high ground for capitalism?

Ludwig von Mises emigrated to the U.S. in 1940. He continued to write and lectured and taught as a visiting professor at N.Y.U. But it was a far cry from his prestige on the continent. Ignored by the media, by the academic community, by business and by government he remained undaunted, a lone figure firm of principle and intellectual courage, a genuine liberal in the classical sense.

Professor von Mises is the painstaking architect of the economy of a free society. However, mainstream economists totally ignore his blueprint. He stands far above the current arguments about how the money supply and the economy should be manipulated. For he maintains our greatest error is for government to exert any influence or control over the supply of money and the economic system.

We ignore Mises' teachings at our own peril and he tells us so. "It rests with men whether they will make the proper use of the rich treasure with which this knowledge provides them or whether they will leave it unused. But if they fail to take the best advantage of it and disregard its teachings and warnings, they will not only annul economics; they will stamp out society and the human race."

CHAPTER FOUR
WHAT COMES AFTER A QUADRILLION?

"Great as our tax burden is, it has not kept pace with public spending. For decades, we have piled deficit upon deficit, mortgaging our future and our children's future for the temporary convenience of the present. To continue this long trend is to guarantee tremendous social, cultural, political, and economic upheavals...It is no coincidence that our present troubles parallel and are proportionate to the intervention and intrusion in our lives that result from unnecessary and excessive growth of government." — Ronald Reagan

"Our whole civilization rests on the fact that men have always succeeded in beating off the attacks of the redistributors." — Ludwig von Mises

Never before has it been clearer that our social and economic future will be disastrous. The trend is not our friend. Most recently our loose money and credit policies created an unsustainable boom that turned into a bust. Attempts to reignite the boom aren't working and the failure of welfarism in Europe threatens to capsize world economies.

It's hard to comprehend the mess we're in. Almost half the people are on some kind of government dole. A significant percentage have character issues that render them unemployable. Entitlement costs are out of control. The big spenders aim to spend more. The welfare state is marching towards bankruptcy and oblivion.

As government deficits rise and the economy stalls money creation will rise dramatically. An economic collapse will be postponed by issuing new money out of thin air. Inevitably this form of counterfeiting will cause goods and services to become shockingly expensive. Since our spending sins are so outrageous the inflationary consequences will be agonizing.

No one ever explained the damage that inflation does like the great Libertarian writer for *Newsweek* and the *New York Times*, Henry Hazlitt (1894 – 1993). He wrote, "When the Federal Reserve banks buy government notes or bonds in the open market, they pay for them, directly or indirectly, by creating money. This is what is known as 'monetizing' the public debt. Inflation goes on as long as this goes on."

The consequences are dire indeed. "Inflation must always end in a crisis and a slump, and worse than the slump itself may be the public delusion that the slump has been caused, not by the previous inflating, but by the inherent defects of a free market."

Hazlitt warned, "It is harmful because it depreciates the value of the monetary unit, raises everybody's cost of living, imposes what is in effect a tax on the poorest... wipes out the value of past savings, discourages future savings, redistributes wealth and income wantonly, encourages and rewards speculation and gambling at the expense of thrift and work, undermines confidence in the justice of a free enterprise system, and corrupts public and private morals."

He continued, "A period of inflation is almost inevitably also a period when demagogy and antibusiness mentality are rampant. If implacable enemies of the country had deliberately set out to undermine and destroy the incentives of the middle classes to work and save, they could hardly have contrived a more effective set of weapons than the present combination of inflation, subsidies, handouts, and confiscatory taxes that our own politicians have imposed upon us."

Mr. Hazlitt explained further, "In a free enterprise system, with an honest and stable money, there is dominantly a close link between effort and productivity on the one hand, and economic reward on the other. Inflation severs this link. Reward comes to depend less and less on effort and production, and more and more on successful gambling and luck."

He continued his litany of warnings, "It is not merely that inflation breeds dishonesty in a nation. Inflation is itself a dishonest act on the part of government, and sets the example for private citizens. When modern governments inflate by increasing the paper-money supply, directly or indirectly, they do in principle what kings once did when they clipped coins. Diluting the money supply with paper is the moral equivalent of diluting the milk supply with water. Notwithstanding all the pious pretenses of governments that inflation is some evil visitation from without, inflation is practically always the result of deliberate governmental policy."

Another excellent economist Hans Sennholz wrote, "If government resorts to inflation, that is, creates money in order to cover its budget deficits or expands credit in order to stimulate business, then no power on earth, no gimmick, device, trick or even indexation can prevent its economic consequences."

In 1931 Mr. Brescioni-Turroni wrote of the Weimar inflation in Germany, "It annihilated thrift... it destroyed incalculable moral and intellectual values. It provoked a serious revolution in social classes, a few people accumulating wealth and forming a class of usurpers of national property, whilst millions of individuals were thrown into poverty. It was a distressing preoccupation and constant torment of innumerable families; it poisoned the German people by spreading among all classes the spirit of speculation and by diverting them from proper and regular work, and it was the cause of incessant political and moral disturbances." That was in 1931, before the hell that followed.

In 1876 Andrew Dickson White wrote of the great French inflation of the 1790's, "With prices soaring and the value of money savings rapidly diminishing, an early effect was the obliteration of thrift. Accompanying this was a cancerous increase in speculation and gambling. Stockjobbing became rife. More and more people began to see the advantages of borrowing and later paying off in depreciated money. A great debtor class grew up whose interest was to keep the inflation going. Workers, finding themselves with less and less real pay in terms of what their wages would buy, while others grew rich by gambling, began to lose interest in steady work. The evaporation of the incomes and savings of the lower and middle classes, and the sudden enrichment of speculators, with their ostentatious luxury, led to mounting social resentment and unrest." Then came Napoleon.

All of this should give you insight into the future. Some of it is already happening. Nobody has ever created as much money out of thin air as the U.S. Soon you'll be hearing the term quadrillion. It's what comes after a trillion. The impact of newly created money generally takes time before it is felt in rising prices. Nor does it hit all goods and services uniformly. Government spokespersons and left wing economists assure us that inflation is not a problem. They are determined to keep on spending. However, price inflation is already worse than the government's statistics indicate.

Going forward it probably won't be too many dollars chasing too few goods that will cause inflation to roar. It's the enormous overabundance of dollars in the world that will strike the dollar down in foreign exchange markets. Because of the European crisis the dollar is getting a boost in demand. That will not last. The trend for the dollar is down. When the dollar declines internationally all commodities rise. They become more expensive. That's where the great inflationary crisis is most likely to strike. Once underway it can turn into massive dollar dumping. In that scenario the government couldn't borrow a dime and only profligate printing would pay the bills. Then you will have to ask, "What comes after a quadrillion?"

CHAPTER FIVE
PAST THE POINT OF NO RETURN

"If the present tax rates had been in effect from the beginning of our century, many who are millionaires today would live under more modest circumstances. But all those new branches of industry which supply the masses with articles unheard of before would operate, if at all, on a much smaller scale, and their products would be beyond the reach of the common man." — Ludwig von Mises

"Of all tyrannies, a tyranny sincerely exercised for the good of its victims may be the most oppressive. It would be better to live under robber barons than under omnipotent moral busybodies." — C.S. Lewis

"Social Security is a fraudulent scheme in which the government collects money from you for your retirement – and immediately spends the money on something else." — Harry Browne

Socialists and progressives are on the march threatening to overturn capitalism and destroy our way of life. We're going down in flames and I don't know if my side is going to win. A huge gulf exists between the left and right that cannot be bridged. You would have to go back to the Civil War to find the kind of intensity, hatred and emotion that exists today. By inciting class warfare politicians have brought the overriding issue of our time to the boiling point.

Will the liberal agenda prevail? We have embraced a great deal of socialism over the past eighty years. It has managed to plunge us deep into debt, debase our currency through inflation, empower government unions, over-regulate, and diminish our freedoms while creating a huge federal bureaucracy that lavishly rewards its employees at the expense of us all. It has created a large and growing population of subsidized citizens who lobby and vote for more money while failing to recognize their dangerous behavioral collapse. For ninety years the left has continuously raised taxes until it has sapped the workers and entrepreneurs of half the rewards of their labor. Then it has managed to spend half again as much like the out of control statist monstrosity that it is.

Our government was originally established to keep the peace, protect us from criminals and maintain a level playing field. Instead of doing a few things well our government insists on doing so many things it does them all badly.

Now the liberals, Socialist and Marxists are on the march. They want more of the same medicine that's ruining us. They want to raise taxes, increase government spending, pass out more subsidies and regulate us into the ground. They want to replace capitalism with some half-baked socialist utopia that has ruined the economy of every country that's fiddled with it. They want no part of free markets and a merit system.

If they prevail (which appears likely) they will plunge us into a new dark age. This is the philosophy that converted Cuba from a prosperous country into a third-world hell-hole. This is a philosophy that praises leftists like Senn Penn for embracing Hugo Chavez and regards the murderous thug Che Guevara as its hero. This is the philosophy that at its extreme murdered one hundred million people in the last century. This is the philosophy that masquerades as social justice by rewarding people for reasons other than hard work and diligence.

We can see it failing in Europe. The 35 hour work weeks, piggish government unions, frequent holidays and long vacations, youthful retirement and useless bureaucracies are killing Europe. In response they run up more debt, inflate, demonstrate, march, riot, and kill a few people. It won't change things. Europe bought into socialism and there's no way out but down.

In many ways the U.S. has set itself up for the same kind of failure. Now when the chickens are coming home to roost a desperate government resorts to the cheap trick of debasing its money and cheating the thrifty. Inflation and socialism feed off one another. Money printing and debt monetization are the left wing's solution to every economic problem. They have the upper hand and they are ruining us.

Now we are at an inflexion point in our economic history. Capitalism is under total assault because a small contingent of fat cats got greased by Uncle Sam. That's what happens when you create money out of thin air. The big banks get the new money first. That's the left's excuse to shove more socialism down our throat. I ask you what chance is there for balanced budgets, limited government, sound money, low taxes, minimal regulation and free markets? Not in my lifetime.

CHAPTER SIX
NO WAY OUT

"The U.S. dollar will be 'devalued' as policy makers seek to weaken it, undermining the greenback's role as an international reserve currency...The dollar is going to lose its status as the world's reserve currency...It will be devalued and it will go down a lot."
— Jim Rogers

"Big government comes at a big cost. This cost most obviously shows in reduced economic growth, fewer jobs, reduced take-home pay, and less overall prosperity. In an era of globalization, when Americans must compete on an international basis, taxation and regulation act as an anchor on American productivity and competitiveness."
— Michael Tanner

Here's just one reason the U.S. has to keep inflating and debasing our currency. Author Richard Mills writes, "The first ever GAO (Government Accountability Office) audit of the U. S. Federal Reserve was recently carried out... What the audit revealed was incredible: between December 2007 and June 2010, the Federal Reserve had secretly bailed out many of the world's banks, corporations, and governments by giving them U.S. $16,000,000,000,000 – that's 16 TRILLION dollars."

Rolling Stone magazine reported, "The Fed sent billions in bailout aid to banks in places like Mexico, Bahrain and Bavaria, billions more to a spate of Japanese car companies, more than $2 trillion in loans each to Citigroup and Morgan Stanley, and billions more to a string of lesser millionaires and billionaires with Cayman Island addresses."

Understand one thing, the U.S. will continue to inflate until it can inflate no more. In order to pay its bills the government creates new dollars and in its fruitless attempt to goose the economy it creates even more new reserves. The Keynesian economists who run our monetary affairs believe that inflating is a sound policy. The *New York Times* columnist Paul Krugman, who does the economic thinking for lockstep liberalism, calls for even more money printing and stimulus. Inflating money and credit are the preferred prescription for the left.

Author Hunter Lewis described John Maynard Keynes' argument: "Full employment should be our goal. The market system will not get us there; it requires government help as well as guidance. This means, in practice, that government will continually print money, in order to reduce interest rates, ultimately to zero, and also borrow and spend as needed. Booms are good, even economic bubbles are acceptable. Recession and bust must be avoided at all cost."

Numerous economists have pointed out that you cannot create wealth and prosperity by printing more money. In fact the boom in housing created by loose money eventually caused a loss of wealth for homeowners. The full employment that Central Bank inflating was supposed to bring about caused just the opposite – high unemployment. These realities are lost on the left. They will say and do anything to keep subsidizing social schemes for their underclass adherents. Deficits don't count with them. No matter what the costs of entitlements and transfer payments they insist they continue come hell or high water. Apparently they never look at the negative results, which among them is the relentless decline in the character of the subsidized.

These entitlements are the chief reason we will inflate into oblivion. Once enacted social schemes like Medicare, Medicaid, food stamps, housing, disability payments, unemployment and welfare are impossible to rescind. They just keep growing. This month $50 billion in Medicare and Medicaid payments will go out. This one area of entitlements threatens all the cost cutting initiatives of Congress. Expensive new drugs, procedures and technologies propel medical costs upwards. The more you subsidize health care the more demand for heath care you get. Adding new health benefits and new beneficiaries ensures that costs can't be controlled. This is the back breaker in the socialist agenda.

Unquestionably we will continue our failing Keynesian monetary prescriptions until the bitter end. A collapse is a certainty. However, deflation and depression will be forestalled by whatever amount of money printing it takes. Ultimately this debasement of our currency will cause price rises that promote panic buying of tangible assets by the public and sets off runaway inflation. A cessation of inflating would cause interest rates to soar, curb lending and choke off economic growth. Either outcome leads to deflation and depression.

Inflating will continue because as the great economic thinker Leonard Read wrote in 1946, "Inflation makes the extension of socialism possible by providing the financial chaos in which it flourishes. The fact is that socialism and inflation are simultaneously cause and effect; they feed on each other."

Despite any talk to the contrary inflating continues today on what author Graham Summers calls a "vertical trajectory." The Fed continues to print money despite the end of QE2. The great economist Irving Fisher (1867 – 1947) wrote, "Irredeemable paper money has almost invariably proved a curse to the country employing it." A curse it will be. When the day comes that we can no longer bail ourselves out through inflating the curse will be in full flower.

What will happen when the government checks purchase little or nothing? What happens when they bounce? What will happen if they are cut by a half or two-thirds? What happens when the welfare transfers end? As we have seen in Madison and Greece no one gets nastier than someone who has had their subsidy taken away. Enjoy the inflating while it lasts. Enjoy the final days of our golden age before it turns into a nightmare. Protect yourself with the knowledge that it must end badly. There's no good way out.

CHAPTER SEVEN
THE GREAT UNTRUTH

"The marketplace is a crime and punishment world, and this Federal Reserve credit expansion is the greatest monetary crime of all time. Accordingly the punishment will be far and away the greatest punishment of all time."
– John Exeter

"The key to growth is quite simple: creative men with money. The cause of stagnation is similarly clear: depriving creative individuals of financial power."
– George Gilder

"Capitalism is what people do if you leave them alone."   – Kenneth Minogue

Three-hundred years ago Emanuel Swedenborg wrote, "It is no proof of man's understanding to be able to affirm whatever he pleases; but to be able to discern that what is true is true, and that what is false is false – this is the mark and character of intelligence." This thought was followed up years later by Ralph Waldo Emerson, "We know truth when we see it, let skeptic and scoffer say what they choose."

Some truths are self-evident. The free market system provides bountiful goods and services. The socialist system brings poverty and stagnation. The great Austrian economist Ludwig von Mises said about free market capitalism, "If you seek [its] monument look around you." Take a moment to reflect on the goods that surround you. Socialism provided none of them.

The entrepreneur Steve Jobs operating within the market system changed our lives. Despite all the evidence liberals and socialists denigrate the free market. They argue for redistribution and a more progressive system. They disdain capitalism. They cannot see the benefits of a free market because their core beliefs are false. They are harbingers of retrogression, poverty, despair and national ruin.

We hear them chatter incessantly about income inequality. They push the idea that the market systems bear responsibility for the rich getting richer while the middle class suffers. In reality it is their socialist schemes and intrusions into the market that have hurt us. They promote big government despite its detrimental impact on our economy. Look at what these liberals have saddled us with. Start with unions. The left passed laws that allowed unions to get a stranglehold on major industries. At one time the auto makers dominated world markets. By 1980 Japanese cars had replaced U.S. cars the world over. Union work rules, lush benefits, impossibly high wages for janitors and other unskilled workers made it easy for the competition to overtake us. Job losses from overseas competitors are enormous.

High taxes, labor unions, trial lawyers, social programs, subsidies and too many regulations kill jobs, growth and wages. All are the policies and building blocks of the left. Worst of all is fiat money. Liberals (Keynesians) promote loose money and credit. It's the reason speculation and financial engineering have overtaken factory production. It's why Wall Street is richer than Main Street. They get the government's newly created money first. It accounts for inequality of incomes and the rich getting richer. The unbridled monetary expansion by government caused the boom and bust we are living through. Yet liberals foster the malicious lie that capitalism and free markets are to blame.

If the left prevails as they have in the past few decades, they will destroy America as we know it. This process has already started. Call it what you will: socialism, liberalism, progressivism, collectivism, we have clear cut proof that it doesn't work. Only go to Cuba or Zimbabwe.

Under socialism, people are equal but only in their poverty and deprivation. The progressive viewpoint is the world's primary falsehood and the path to economic purgatory and social hell. Time is running out on the truth.

CHAPTER EIGHT
HE COULD SEE THE FUTURE

"In the transfer society, the general public is not only poorer but also less contented, less autonomous, more rancorous, and politicized. Individuals take part less often in voluntary community activities and more often in belligerent political contests. Genuine communities cannot breathe in the poisonous atmosphere of redistributional politics." – Robert Higgs

"The state is a force incarnate. Worse, it is the silly parading of force. It never seeks to prevail by persuasion. Whenever it thrusts its finger into anything, it does so in the most unfriendly way. Its essence is command and compulsion." – Michael Bakunin

We call it the housing bubble but really it was the greatest money and credit excess in the history of the world. The immense damage to our economy from the bursting of this bubble continues to haunt us. How is it that a calamity of this magnitude could not be foreseen by our political leadership, our economists, our so-called wizards of Wall Street and all the other experts?

A few people saw it coming. Twenty years ago in 1991, I had been writing about the perils of credit excess and big government for almost two decades. However, what I warned about never seemed to happen. I sounded like a broken record. Eventually, I came across an interview in a newsletter with a German economist by the name of Kurt Richebacher. He was a financial forecaster who was influenced by Austrian School economics. I called him on the phone and over time we became friends. At that time Kurt was the only significant economist that predicted a dire financial outcome.

As far back as 1996 he was warning about a stock market crash. "The bullish wave threatens to come crashing down on the hordes of analysts and investors who bet so heavily – and so foolishly – on their dreams of a perpetual 'stock market boom.'"

In 1999 he wrote, "The U.S. financial system today hangs in an increasingly precarious position, a house of cards literally built on nothing but financial leverage, speculation and derivatives."

As the Nasdaq bubble deflated he wrote in June of 2000, "The decisive cause of every single, serious economic and currency crisis are credit and debt excesses. Apparently, we cannot repeat it often enough: the U.S. credit and debt excesses of the past few years are beyond past experience in history, essentially leaving behind a totally vulnerable economy and financial system."

One of his sternest warnings came in 1999 when he criticized Alan Greenspan for his speech endorsing derivatives. "To be the leading Central banker of the world, it really ought to be obvious that the overriding consequences of widespread derivatives use is excessive leverage and risk taking... derivatives markets encourage a dangerous shifting of risk to parties with less wherewithal to shoulder potential losses. This is particularly the case during an acute financial crisis precisely when derivative 'insurance' is called for. We see... massive shifting of market risk to the highly leveraged and exposed U.S. banking industry and Wall Street firms."

In 2002 he warned about the collapse of national savings, "The total carnage of national savings is the U.S. economy's most important – but also most widely ignored predicament... national savings have been squandered to pay for spending that the consumer cannot afford from his current income."

He continued with a crucial economics lesson, one that the Keynesians have totally failed to grasp. "Ever since Adam Smith, savings has meant exactly one and the same thing in all languages: it is the part of current income that is not spent on consumption. And the key point of this definition is that such savings, and such savings only, make it possible to divert real resources from the production of consumption goods to the production of capital goods.

"To pin down and emphasize the key point: savings from current income represent the economy's supply of capital. Thus, it definitely sets the limits to the financial funds and the real resources that are available for new capital investment. Any increase in consumer spending as a share of GDP correspondingly decreases the economy's capacity for capital formation. It is, of course, easy to replace missing savings with credit creation. But there is no substitute for missing real resources.

"In the end it is all about capital investment. It is the critical mass in the process of economic growth that generates all the things that make for rising wealth and living standards. Capital investment creates demand, growing supply, employment, productivity, income, profits and tangible wealth."

He concluded, "The crucial thing to see about the U.S. economy is that its growth during the past few years was driven by uncontrolled debt creation for consumption and financial speculation, while in the process domestic savings and the potential for capital investment have been devastated as never before... The first thing to get straight is that this was – and still is – the most outrageous bubble economy in history, far worse than the U.S. bubble of the 1920s and Japan's bubble of the late 1980s." (Remember, this was 2002.)

"Very few people so far have realized that the U.S. economy is sick to the bone. In the past few years it has been grossly mismanaged, on the macro level through unprecedented monetary looseness on the part of the Greenspan Fed, and on the micro level through corporate strategies that built only mountains of financial leveraging but no factories."

In 2005, he delivered this indictment of the U.S. economy. "The ongoing credit explosion is financing a lot of different things, except production and tangible capital formation. Debt growth is almost entirely used for unproductive purposes, such as consumption, imports, government deficits, purchases of existing assets and financial speculation."

He continued, "Credit growth in the United States has gone completely insane. This is sheer Ponzi financing – and like all Ponzi schemes someone will end up holding the bag. At the same time, the diversion of credit into bonds, stock and housing has created an illusion of bulging wealth.

"This so called wealth creation has its quack origins in loose money and artificially low interest rates; it boosts consumption at the expense of saving and investment. Strictly speaking, this is the exact opposite of wealth creation – impoverishment."

By 2006 Kurt Richebacher was warning about a pending downturn. "The U.S. economy is in danger of a recession that will prove unusually severe and long...The great question is what will happen to the variety of financial asset bubbles in the United States when the housing bubble bursts and the economy slumps."

In the spring of 2007 Kurt Richebacher suddenly lost his eyesight. In our last conversation I could hear the anguish in his voice as he explained to me that he had gone permanently blind. To someone who spent much of their time reading financial reports and economic statistics this was devastating beyond measure. Soon afterwards Kurt Richebacher passed away.

In one of his final newsletters in January of 2007 he wrote with amazing prescience, "In our view, the obvious major risk is in the impending bust of the gigantic housing bubble. Home ownership is broadly spread among the population, in contrast to owning stocks. So the breaking of the housing bubble will hurt the American people far more than did the collapse in stock prices in 2000 – 2002... Someday, the same will happen to the bond and stock market... Another big risk is the dollar."

It's sad that Kurt Richenbacher did not live to see the sorry outcome of the monetary excesses he warned about. The accuracy of his predictions makes him the soothsayer of the century. The economist Paul Krugman argued in 2002 that the Federal Reserve should do what it could to create a housing bubble; yet, he received a Nobel Prize. Nobody paid much attention to Kurt Richebacher and his accurate forecasts. In a rational world Kurt Richebacher would have won the Nobel and Krugman would have been fired.

Were he alive I'm sure Kurt Richebacher would agree with my view that Paul Krugman, from his influential post at the *New York Times* is the most dangerous and wrong thinking economist since Karl Marx. Kurt would also have pilloried Mr. Bernanke just as he did Mr. Greenspan. He would argue that the politicians and monetary authorities in charge today suffer a profound economic ignorance. He would agree, they are leading us into catastrophe. He would be warning us about a falling dollar, a bursting bond bubble, a gathering recession and wrong-headed policy prescriptions coming from Washington. He would agree we could not be in worse hands.

CHAPTER NINE
NONE ARE SO BLIND

"Recipients of transfer set a bad example for others, including their children, other relatives, and friends, who see that one can receive goods, services or money from the government without earning them. The onlookers easily adopt an attitude rking, self-reliant people in their families or neighborhoods."
– Robert Higgs

"I cannot lay my finger on that article of the Constitution which granted a right to Congress of expending, on objects of benevolence, the money of their constituents."
– James Madison

Whether in Europe or America, if those who misbehave are part of the subsidized underclass, they're excused as victims. In Toronto, Canada six shootings in 24 hours recently made the headlines. Former mayor, John Sewell, obviously a liberal, claimed that much of the violence stems from "treating black kids in a way that has made them give up generally on the traditional roots we have for success in this society... We've got to rush in with big programs quickly."

That's the liberal mantra; if people misbehave, rush in with programs that give them more money. But, big social programs cause more problems than they cure. Years ago, management guru Peter Drucker summed it up: "Despite ever larger and constantly growing expenditures, the 'welfare mess' in the United States is getting steadily worse. In fact, a strong case can be made - and has been made - that the poor in America... have become the poorer, the more helpless, the more disadvantaged, the more welfare money is being spent to help them. American welfare spending encourages dependence. It paralyzes rather than energizes."

Why is it that proponents of subsidies never catch on to the error of their ways? Why don't they see the harm in giving people money they didn't earn? It's really not that hard to figure out why people who are subsidized misbehave. They don't have anything to do. The operative word is boredom.

In 1966, Robert Ardrey wrote a controversial inquiry into the nature of man entitled, *The Territorial Imperative*. He theorized that there are three principal needs of all higher animals, including man: the need for identity, the need for stimulation and the need for security. Ardrey wrote, "Identity, stimulation, security; if you will think of them in terms of their opposites their images will be sharpened. Identity is the opposite of anonymity. Stimulation is the opposite of boredom. Security is the opposite of anxiety. We shun anonymity, dread boredom, seek to dispel anxiety. We grasp at identification, yearn for stimulation, conserve or gain security."

"There are few exceptions," he wrote, "To the rule that the need for identity is the most powerful and most pervasive among all species. The need for stimulation is not far behind. And security, normally, will be sacrificed for either of the other two." Then, ominously for the welfare state he wrote, "The structure of security is the birthplace of boredom...our means of satisfying innate needs are precious few, and sacrifice of any must mean replacement by another."

The universal requirement to feed, clothe and shelter ourselves fulfills many of the human needs Ardrey wrote about. Work relieves boredom, and even a humdrum job brings far more stimulation than idleness. Success at a job brings status and identity that relieves anonymity. And security is (by definition) the result of work and labor.

Social welfare provides security, but deprives the recipient of the stimulation and identity that come from work and struggle. Writing in a biology book in the mid-60s, almost as though he could foretell the failed future of "The Great Society," Robert Ardrey stated, "We may agree, for example, that our societies must provide greater security for the individual; yet if all we succeed in producing is a social structure providing increased anonymity and ever increasing boredom, then we should not wonder if ingenious man turns to such amusements as drugs, housebreaking, vandalism, mayhem, riots, or - at the most harmless - strange haircuts, costumes, standards of cleanliness, and sexual experiments." Nowhere else has anyone written a more apt description of the welfare predicament.

Work is part of the growth process of life. A job forces people to maintain certain standards of good character, effort and temperance. If you steal, lie or take drugs while at work, you lose your job. Subsidies do not weaken you so much as excuse you from the normal pressures of employment and self sufficiency that make you stronger, and improve your character.

The time is overdue for society to conclude that human nature does not harmonize with income supports. The longer people receive economic assistance, the worse their social condition and behavior. Welfare reform has been undermined by numerous subsidies and a relaxation of the rules. Now the subsidized underclass is growing as much as three times faster than the general population. Where's it going to end?

Jobs are available despite claims to the contrary. All too often unemployment is used as an excuse for misbehaving when jobs are within walking distance. At the very least, people who get subsidies should have to get up in the morning and do something, even if it's a make work job. But most liberals would oppose even this simple test of responsibility.

CHAPTER TEN
VOICE IN THE WILDERNESS

Capitalism is a belief that nobody is wise enough and knows enough to control the lives of other people. When each person busy, sells, consumes, produces, saves, and spends at will, the 'miracle of the market' enables everyone to benefit."
– Perry Gresham

"Inflation gradually pushes the whole community towards speculation, since ordinary life begins to require speculator's skills." — William Rees-Mogg

"What the political left, even in democratic countries, share is the notion that knowledgeable and virtuous people like themselves have both a right and a duty to use the power of government to impose their superior knowledge and virtue on others." — Thomas Sowell

One of the smartest men who lived in the twentieth century was Leonard Read (1898 – 1983). He was a Libertarian social and economic philosopher with a profound insight into the damning effect of socialism and inflation. Naturally, he was ignored by the media. Nevertheless, in a half dozen short books this kind and gentle man demolished modern liberalism and big government on the basis of its morality.

He saw that government resorted to force and coercion to take the earnings of unwilling citizens. He knew that if you don't pay taxes someone from the government will eventually come with a gun. Many years ago they came to my company with their guns so I know it to be true. Mr. Read's condemnation was harsh. He said there was no moral difference between a pickpocket and a tax collector. He condemned coercion as destructive to freedom. To him forcing citizens to do what they otherwise would not do if left alone was a form of extortion. He called it socialized dishonesty.

This coercion Leonard Read railed against had consequences. Since it was an evil act it would bring retribution. Only bad could come from it. He claimed there was no greater dishonesty than feathering one's nest at the expense of another. He insisted that no person could benefit by living off this confiscated income. It would not improve one's character or growth. To live on the money that government provided was as evil as them taking it in the first place. He saw a terrible end for those who lived on other people's earnings.

What's happening today bears him out. The more money we give to the subsidized the more money they demand and the worse they behave. The more entitlements they receive the more they feel entitled to them. We even hear vague threats to our safety if they don't get a bigger cut. We hear endless complaints about the raw deal our society gives the welfare class. To add insult to injury those who the government takes the most from are vilified and cursed. The most affluent taxpayers who finance the bulk of the welfare payments are hated because they supposedly don't pay enough. Leonard Read was right to argue that this process could only have a bad ending.

Of the tax collectors, government regulators and bureaucrats he wrote, "I cannot indulge in my own upgrading at the same time I am inhibiting someone else's creative action. Therefore, to the extent that one's life is spent in using force to coerce others, to that extent is one's life destroyed and its higher purpose frustrated...Nothing creative is induced by compulsion."

Leonard Read suggested that private charity was instrumental in making a society great. Under capitalism the charitable acts of private individuals would grow and flourish thus eliminating many of societies' ills. But with income redistribution these bonds of brotherhood are crushed by government compulsion. Bureaucrats decide who gets what at the expense of private giving and charity. This kind of socialism, he suggested, would cause our nation to "fly apart."

Because socialism relies on compulsion, Leonard Read stood firmly against it. He wrote, "Socialism takes and redistributes wealth, but it is utterly incapable of creating wealth." He warned, "Man cannot feign the role of God without finally playing the devil's part." His most profound criticism of government regarded its constant inflating. "Inflation makes the extension of socialism possible by providing the financial chaos in which it flourishes. The fact is that socialism and inflation are simultaneously cause and effect; they feed on each other!"

As if firing a warning across the bow of Washington and Wall Street he quoted a wise man. "Ultimately with God's aid, truth always emerges and finally prevails supreme in its power over the destiny of mankind, and terrible is the retribution for those who deny, defy, or betray it." That's how Leonard Read saw it. Big government and socialism would cause our economy to disintegrate. Unfortunately, this nearsighted nation ignores any such warnings.

CHAPTER ELEVEN
HERO TO THE LEFT

"People try to live within their income so they can afford to pay taxes to a government that can't live within its income." — Robert Half

"The essential quality of a free economy is that it cannot be planned. It leaves the solution of problems to the inspiration of the individuals in the untrammeled population. When something approaching a free economy has existed, it has always worked better than the schemes of any planners." — Thomas H. Berber

"Few policies are more calculated to destroy the existing basis of a free society than the debauching of its currency. And few tasks, if any, are more important to the champion of freedom that creation of a sound monetary system." — Hans F. Sennholz

For the most part, liberals in America take their economic cues from *New York Times* columnist Paul Krugman. From his post at the Times the Keynesian Krugman promotes socialized health care, higher taxes, massive government spending and a vastly bigger stimulus package. He's way to the left of the new administration when it comes to spending (if that's possible).

The far left in this country has limited economic insight on the origins of prosperity. You really have to wonder about Mr. Krugman when he writes that capitalism is inhumane and the free market is amoral. It escapes him that wherever it has been practiced, capitalism eliminated starvation, rolled back disease and dramatically improved living standards. As economist Lewellyn Rockwell puts it, "The market economy has created unfathomable prosperity and, decade-by-decade, century-by-century, miraculous feats of innovation, production, distribution, and social coordination. To the free market, we owe all material prosperity, all leisure time, our health and longevity, our huge and growing population and nearly everything we call life itself."

I'm afraid most of the Keynesians running our country don't have any more understanding about wealth creation than does Mr. Krugman when he writes, "Nobody really knows why the U.S. economy could generate 3 percent annual productivity growth before 1973 and only 1 percent afterward; nobody really knows why Japan surged from defeat to global economic power after World War II, while Britain slid slowly into third-rate status." Believe it or not, they don't know that low taxes, less regulation, sound money, high savings and a market economy free of exchange controls, powerful labor unions, welfarism and bureaucracy will experience rapid growth. Rather, they see injustice because everybody's economic outcomes are not the same. It drives them crazy that paupers and poets don't get the same share as successful entrepreneurs.

We are in real danger when an influential, Nobel Prize winning liberal economist can write that we "don't know how to make a poor country rich or bring back the magic of economic growth when it seems to have gone away." It's certainly true that the liberals in Washington don't know how to invigorate our economy. In fact, if the politicians continue to follow Mr. Krugman's advice, we can throw in the towel on the economy.

It's not that hard. Adam Smith summed it up. "Little else is required to carry a state to the highest degree of opulence from the lowest barbarism; but peace, easy taxes and a tolerable administration of justice." Or how about Ben Franklin: "In short, the way to wealth, if you desire it, is as plain as the way to market. It depends chiefly on two words, industry and frugality." Economist Ludwig von Mises sums up what Keynesians and liberals never seem to understand regarding the need for savings. "A country becomes more prosperous in proportion to the rise in the invested capital per unit of its population."

The reason that liberalism is so dangerous to America is that they never learn from their failures (welfarism) or from the successes of capitalism. Newsletter editor Bill Buckler writes about one such triumph. "In the aftermath of WWII, large parts of Germany were little more than piles of rubble or smoking ashes. Most of their major cities had been all but destroyed by bombing. Their infrastructure and transportation links lay in ruins. The nation itself was fully occupied by the conquering powers and in the process of being split in half with the eastern half swallowed by USSR-sponsored totalitarianism.....

"The Germans themselves were utterly demoralised, having lost a world war for the second time in one generation. What economic exchange there was took place by means of barter. Cigarettes were used as money for those who had no access to the 'scrip' issued by the occupying powers...'Aid' did not resuscitate the western half of Germany - a return to sound economics and (relatively) sound money did.

"The process was simplicity itself. In one move over a long weekend in mid-1948, the German government...[abolished] controls on prices and wages and [lifted] most of the regulatory structure on the economy...The next day, the German people almost literally began to construct a new nation out of the rubble. Inside of a decade, Germany had one of the most dynamic and richest economies in the world and a currency which was arguably the soundest in the world.

"In the words of the great Austrian Economist, Wilhelm Roepke, advisor to German Economics Minister Ludwig Erhard at the time: '...here is to be found the most convincing case in all history against collectivism and inflationism and for market economy and monetary discipline.'"

Rather than adopt the free market economic policies that have time and again proven their merit, Mr. Krugman espouses socialistic schemes that have never worked. As Winston Churchill once quipped, "The inherent vice of capitalism is the unequal sharing of blessings; the inherent virtue of socialism is the equal sharing of misery."

The essence of our contemporary application of Keynesian economics is best described by analyst Michael Metrosky. "Spend all the money you have. When you run out of money, borrow all you can and spend that too. When nobody will loan you any more money, just print the money and keep spending." It's a fitting epitaph for an economy in the process of being killed by the likes of Mr. Krugman, the *New York Times* and the Keynesians in Washington who have been in charge over the past five administrations.

CHAPTER TWELVE
NO ONE'S LISTENING

"What made some enterprises develop into 'big business' was precisely their success in filling best the demands of the masses."   – Ludwig von Mises

"So much debt has been created in the last twenty years that it requires huge amounts of new credit simply to keep the system liquid. The necessity for ever-larger amounts of credit to keep the system liquid weighs on the ability of the Fed to reflate. It's like pouring more and more water in the bathtub with a big hole in the bottom."   – Dan Denning

"Today it is not big business that we have to fear. It big government."   – Wendell Phillips

The acid test of intelligence is whether the things you believe in turn out to be true. Thus it's always good to periodically examine one's premises. I regularly immerse myself in the books of the Austrian School economists, Ludwig von Mises, Murray Rothbard and Nobel prize winner Friedrich Hayek. It's made me more certain than ever that we, as a nation, have drifted so far from rational economic moorings that a monumental financial disorder cannot be avoided.

Today, Austrian economics remains a little known economic school. Contemporary economists totally ignore the Austrian school, and question the sanity of anyone who would use this obscure philosophy as the springboard for views that predict financial catastrophe. Nevertheless, Austrian school thinking, however unfashionable, has an impressive intellectual history. For example, economists from Adam Smith to Karl Marx believed that the value of a thing was determined by the amount of labor that went into making it. Thus Marx could claim that, since laborers created the value of things, they were due all the profits and capitalists were cheating them. "Workers of the world unite." From this premise spread the disruptive Marxist philosophy which, at times, seemed to own the world (especially intellectuals within the United States).

However, in Austria a professor of economics (Eugen Bohm-Bawerk) developed a different explanation of how a thing got value. He knew that ten thousand men could labor to build a pyramid and no one would pay anything for it. But pick up a diamond off an Arkansas hillside and you could sell it for $10,000. Why was gold worth more than silver, which was more useful to industry? This was the paradox of value which no economist could resolve.

Bohm-Bawerk knew that you and other consumers are the true arbiters of value. You choose whether an item has value to you. Value is subjective. If you have three wagon loads of grain to last you the winter and you plan to eat one load, use another for seed and feed the birds with the other, you would naturally price them differently. You would trade the third load for much less than the second. The last (or most recent) sale you make of a bag of grain from your wagon is the present value. It's called marginal-utility. The bag with the least marginal-utility (value to you) sets the value.

The Austrians solved the value paradox by stating that *you don't value the entire world supply of an item, but only a given supply which you can use at that moment.* This brilliant analysis became the accepted economic alternative to the value theory of Marxist economists, and the core of Austrian economic theory. Economics professor Hans Sennholz states that the Austrians "Thereby managed to place the individual in the center of their analysis and the consumer at the core of the economic order."

Socialists want the state to determine price and value; the Austrians know that only the individual can accomplish this. The buying choices of the individual make the world go round, and this free choice is basic to our liberty. The buying choice of the consumer determines profit and loss and the success and failure of businesses and products.

CHAPTER THIRTEEN
HOW WE GOT HERE

*"Because an inflationary policy works only as long as the yearly increments
in the amount of money in circulation are increased more and more, the rise in
prices and wages and the corresponding drop in purchasing power will go on at
an accelerated pace."*
                                                           – Ludwig von Mises

*"For some reason, our media are fascinated by stories that appear to harm
American national interests."*
                                                           – Bob Tyrell

How did our country drift so far towards big government and socialism? It
was never this way. Throughout my lifetime we kept moving leftward embracing one government program after another. In my family we listened to the
national news every night at 5:30 P.M. Edward R. Murrow, Walter Cronkite,
Huntley and Brinkley fed us a steady diet promoting big government and
undermining capitalism. The major networks were all left-leaning and the
newspapers and magazines were even more liberal. Big city dailies like the
New York Times and *Washington Post* published the progressive agenda and
magazines like *Time* and *Newsweek* became rabid advocates of government
solutions. Unfortunately, none have ever confronted the massive failures they
engineered.

For years the media fed us left-wing prescriptions. It influenced a lot of people. They are still at it. They stump for liberal politicians and promote leftist
personalities. Recently Warren Buffet has been getting a lot of ink. Why? He
came out for raising taxes. That's the way it works. You get your book re-
viewed if you are a liberal. You get your art praised if you are a socialist. Why
is it that most high-buck modern artists are leftists? The liberal media helped
them succeed. I wonder if a right wing artist exists.

Over the years, every silly socialist scheme drew praise while practical market
solutions were ignored. So we embraced all the big programs and now we're
going broke. There's no way we can pay for our government's wasteful spending. Costs are out of control because social programs are open-ended. They
only grow. Unfortunately this runaway spending aggravates the problems they
are supposed to cure thus requiring even more spending. Our trillion dollar
deficits and our unfunded budget liabilities in the mega-trillions tell the whole
story. We are ultimately facing national bankruptcy or total dollar debasement.

Our shrinking economy means you can't pay the bills by raising taxes and liberal social sympathy rules out any spending cuts.

Financial survival in the environment that big government liberals have created is more dicey than ever. In July of 2008 I wrote an article that tried to get across the peril that we all face. One paragraph stands out.

"Eighty years ago, in 1928, Babe Ruth, the greatest baseball player of all time, made $50,000 a year. Alex Rodriguez, a Yankee star of today, makes $28 million. The Babe made 1/5 of 1% of Rodriguez's salary. That's .002. In a way, you could say the money of 1928 has become virtually worthless.

"Let's go back 40 years – half way to 1928. In 1968 Willie Mays was voted the Most Valuable Player in the All Star game. He made $120,000 that year. Do you 'get it?' $50,000 - $120,000 - $28,000,000. The rate of depreciation of the dollar is increasing exponentially (the bigger it gets, the faster it grows). Somewhere in America today (or in South America), a two year old kid tosses around a rubber ball. In less than 30 years he will earn one billion dollars a year to play ball."

Maybe it will be a trillion. You can't look at the inflation rate month to month or even year to year. Look at it over five to ten year periods and you see how insidious it is. Wall Street and Washington have been telling us there's low inflation for decades. It is getting tougher and tougher for young people to get married and raise a family because inflation is far worse than the government tells us. Wages can't keep up. Millions of young people now turn to the government to subsidize their food or rent. Inflation leaves a country in financial ruin. Our government relies on blatant money creation and raw inflating to pay for the socialist monstrosity it has created. We don't know the timing of our future downfall but we do know that big government not only doesn't work it brings a nation to its knees.

CHAPTER FOURTEEN
ANTI-CAPITALIST

"Capitalism encourages entrepreneurs to act with consideration for others even when their ultimate motive is to benefit themselves." – Dinesh D'Souza

"The market is color-blind." – W.H. Hutt

I'm dismayed by the current level of hatred directed towards capitalism. In my lifetime I've never heard such expressions of bitterness. This is the consequence of left-wing professors and the liberal media poisoning the well. Liberal parents have managed to turn their offspring into good little Marxists or at least into people who share Marxist animosity towards free markets and capitalism. They grossly exaggerate the so-called sins of capitalism and believe any canard no matter how baseless. Here is an example in a recent email I received, followed by my reply.

Mr. Cook,

It's very tiring to constantly read your apologetic definition of successful corporations and capitalists as having got that way "because they did a superior job of meeting the product needs of the people in the best, most economical way. The hallmark of big business is mass production for the benefit of the masses."

Nonsense. The most successful ones – and rightly the ones most despised – got that way because of their ruthless, "no holds barred" mindset. Ever hear of the robber barons? How about Bill Gates and all the anti-competitive lawsuits Microsoft defended itself against?

Let's not forget Merck, who waited for years and thousands of deaths from the known side effects of Vioxx before pulling it from the market. All that happens to such companies is a piddling fine (in reality, out of shareholder dividends) that are hardly a slap on the wrist. Meanwhile, they keep the billions in profits and the lowlife, responsible decision makers get rewarded with big bonuses, options, etc. and are not held accountable (no personal financial fines or jail time).

Statin drugs have never been proven to be of benefit for women; yet they are still promoted. The seasonal and H1N1 flu vaccines are another scam, but the government goes along with it since they are owned by the drug companies, and will do anything to ensure their profits, which in turn keeps the campaign contributions coming in.

You said that the hallmark of big business is mass production for the benefit of the masses. How do the masses benefit from hedge funds? From day-trading speculators, who boost prices of such things as oil well above their supply-demand value? From the trash running Goldman Sachs and the rest responsible for the global meltdown? From when companies dump untreated toxic waste into streams and rivers, all to save a buck...I can go on for pages, but what's the use. I can't tell if you are too blind to acknowledge these realities about capitalism, or you think your readers are so stupid that we believe your idealistic fairy tales.

Ron,

People on the left are great at digging up 10 or 15 companies as examples of abuses. But, what about the millions of companies (like mine) who provide valuable products and services without any kind of problems. Without them we would still be living in caves. Despite your dislike these corporations have rescued us from disease and starvation and provide us with goods and luxuries that make our modern life what it is.

Socialism on the other hand has invented or created nothing. There is no alternative to capitalist abundance but socialist poverty and misery. That is the unarguable lesson of economic history.

Jim Cook

Ron jumps to the conclusion that Wall Street rather than Washington was responsible for the mortgage mess. The left never sees the government at fault for anything. He trots out that old bugaboo about the robber barons. Does he mean Rockefeller who pushed down the price of oil so people could afford it? Maybe, he means Henry Ford who built automobiles for the masses or Carnegie who made steel widely available and spent his fortune building public libraries. He even defames Bill Gates. Capitalism is evil because of Bill

Gates? Maybe he should move to Cuba. They don't have modern electronics there so you can't blame Microsoft for anything.

Such exaggeration. Is any company dumping untreated toxic waste into a river these days? Not unless they want a lawsuit and a jail term. Are drug companies purposely selling unproven or harmful drugs that kill people? What a jaundiced view of humanity.

Believe it or not, speculation, market making, trading and hedging serve to make prices orderly and less expensive. When it doesn't happen that way it's generally because someone is getting around the law. It's our government's role to protect us from outside enemies, domestic criminals, law breakers and con artists. There are going to be crooks under capitalism, just as there are crooks within the government. The Madoffs and the manipulators are examples of government regulatory failures. Don't blame capitalism. If you're looking for crimes and horror stories look at socialism. It managed to murder 100 million people in the last century.

What is it with today's liberals mouthing Marxist platitudes and anti-capitalist drivel? They are the worst mealy-mouthed do-gooders in history. Their bumbling, exorbitantly expensive attempts at social justice have had a ruinous impact on the recipients of this welfare. Their constant engineering of higher taxes and easy money has wrecked the economy. Their subsidies have convoluted markets and put their foolish energy fads ahead of practical solutions. Their liberal agenda is the blueprint for national ruin. On top of these colossal failures they have the nerve to condemn capitalism.

CHAPTER FIFTEEN
JOB CREATION

"The solution to our problems is not more paternalism, laws, decrees, and controls, but the restoration of liberty and free enterprise, the restoration of incentives, to let loose the tremendous constructive energies of 300 million Americans."
— Henry Hazlitt

"One of the myths that everyone is taught is that the government has some sort of tremendous understanding of economics and the ability to make adjustments to economic activity. The term fine-tuning is used sometimes. Actually, we are talking about a group of human beings who don't know much more about real economics than anybody else. They think they do, but they don't. They just bounce around from one attempt to control things to the next, making a mess of the country."
— Charles Smith

I started Investment Rarities in 1973. We had a brief run in 1974 when gold and silver jumped up but by 1975 it was over. The first energy crisis had dawned and we survived by developing and selling the Sierra Wood Burning Stove. We began to publish the *Wood Burning Quarterly* publication, which sold in fireplace stores. In time, we changed the name to *Home Energy Digest* and wrote extensively about solar energy, wind power, biomass and other forms of alternative energy. The government was pouring money into all of them in the form of grants, subsidies and tax breaks. Nothing much came of it. The government wasted a lot of money.

One day I got a call from an engineer who read our magazine. He made an appointment to see me. During his visit he explained that he and 70 others were being paid by the government to come up with solutions to the energy crisis. It had been two years and thus far they hadn't hit upon anything. My advice was to develop an energy-saving product that people would buy. Apparently that had never dawned on them because he thought it was a great idea. My distaste for government solutions went up a notch after this meeting. I knew they would never come up with anything and the government was wasting money on endless projects like this across the nation. Today they are force feeding billions to create green jobs. I've seen this act before. It doesn't work.

The government thinks if they take enough money from the people who earn it and subsidize a bunch of people this will create millions of jobs. How dumb are they? Let me tell you what it takes to create jobs. Someone has to turn their back on their financial security, step away from a regular paycheck and risk everything on a business venture. They have to undergo days and nights of wracking anxiety, work and struggle for months without gain and skirt the edge of failure while finding the will to persist.

If they can survive this relentless adversity and be creative enough to develop a product or service that people want they can begin to break even and eventually hire someone. That creates one job. No matter how many employees a company eventually has, that's how it starts. Is there anyone in Washington who understands what it takes to create one job?

For every new business that succeeds there are fifty that don't last five years. Those who survive and begin to make a profit are in for a rude awakening. The precious capital they've managed to earn gets quickly taxed away by the government. This is money that would otherwise be used to create growth and employment. A business strives to gain a financial cushion that will help them survive a slump or downturn. However, state and federal taxes take half of their profits thereby stunting employment and killing jobs.

There's a formula for job creation. Let businesses keep more of what they earn. Most especially let business startups go without taxes. For an immediate turnaround cut all business taxes to the bone. Make it highly profitable to take risks that create jobs. Unleash the entrepreneurs and get the government out of the way.

CHAPTER SIXTEEN
PENALTY ON PROGRESS

"People who make more are taxed more. That's being punished for being more productive. And then you're being rewarded for being a parasite. If you don't do anything, if you're just a bum, why, you can go on relief. You get something for nothing. That's a violation of rationality and morality in the short run too. The less you do, the more you get. The more you do, the more you're punished. That's a fine standard for a culture! The most productive people are punished the most for being productive; the ones who produce the least are rewarded for being parasites. Now, if I tried to design an irrational structure of a society, this is exactly what I'd pick." – Andrew J. Galambos

"Taxing the rich to fund poorly managed government programs is simply a self-destructive decision: It does nothing more than move money and investment decisions away from proven moneymakers (read: job producers) to Washington amateurs. In both cases, Americans lose." – T. J. Rodgers

"There is no – let me repeat – no example in the last quarter-century of a large complex economy that has been successful with high taxes." – Jonah Goldberg

In the winter I spend some time on a little island in southwest Florida. This tropical paradise runs seven miles long and is two blocks wide. A small toll bridge connects it to the mainland. For the most part, the four thousand residents (in peak season) are wealthy. One or two are in the Forbes 400.

Every morning a constant stream of autos and trucks cross onto the island. They contain people who work on the homes and the yards of the affluent. This constant flow of carpenters, maids, plumbers, landscapers, air conditioning contractors, handymen, pool cleaners, security guards, repairmen, cable guys, gardeners and decorators make their livelihood off the rich. When taxes are raised on the wealthy, fewer of these workers will be employed.

Left-wing schemes to raise taxes to 60% are aimed exclusively at high-income earners. This money will supposedly go to equalize the low incomes of the subsidized underclass. The late economist, Murray Rothbard, had this to say about this tax gouging. "The modern welfare state, highly touted as soaking the rich to subsidize the poor, does no such thing. In fact, soaking the rich would have disastrous effects, not just for the rich but for the poor and middle class themselves. For it is the rich who provide a proportionately greater amount of saving, investment capital, entrepreneurial foresight, and financing of technological innovation, that has brought the United States to by far the highest standard of living – for the mass of the people – of any country in history."

Rich people and people attempting to get rich create the jobs. Unemployment will rise when taxes are increased. If you want to impoverish the populace of a country, tax the rich out of existence. In that way you can turn the country into a third world hellhole. There are no millionaires in Bangladesh or similar economic backwaters. The more millionaires and billionaires in a country, the higher the standard of living. All the former communist countries have learned this lesson. They continue to push tax rates lower towards 10%. Their economies are booming. Eventually their standard of living will pass ours.

Our liberals and progressives want to raise taxes and pass out money to alleviate income inequality. Unfortunately, this redistribution scheme does just the opposite. It makes everybody worse off. Taking money from those who earned it for the government to waste on a myriad of follies reduces our national wealth and prosperity.

The emotional mix of envy and altruism, which comprises modern liberalism, pays no heed to century-old lessons of economics. Rather, it relies on socialist misconceptions. The liberal tax agenda is the harbinger of economic retrogression and national failure. Every citizen at every economic level will suffer because of it.

CHAPTER SEVENTEEN
HOLLYWOOD HORRORS

"For members of the political class, the crucial question is always: how can we push out the frontier, how can we augment the government's dominion and plunder, with net gain to ourselves, the exploiters who live not by honest production and voluntary exchange, but by fleecing those who do so?" – Robert Higgs

"The profit system balances human needs with the availability of all the world's resources, unleashes the amazing power of human creativity, and works to meet the material needs of every member of society at the least possible cost. It does this through exchange, cooperation, competition, entrepreneurship, and all the institutions that make possible capitalism – the most productive economic system this side of heaven." – Llewellyn H. Rockwell, Jr.

A few years ago a new version of the film, "Manchurian Candidate," replaced the old movie's Korean War villains with a new set of wrongdoers, the managers of a mutual fund. It was totally preposterous. The evil company, Manchurian Equities, implants devices in the brains of innocent soldiers to make them kill the newly elected U.S. president. The old movie was good, but the goofy addition of an equity fund as the villain ruins the new movie. The Hollywood left insists on painting business persons as arch criminals, even though it's ridiculous. They like to depict free enterprise, capitalism and business leaders as sources of evil and criminality. Somehow they think that will influence enough people to further their left-wing agenda.

If it would do any good, someone should read them Llewellyn Rockwell, Jr.'s case for capitalism. "The market economy has created unfathomable prosperity and, decade by decade, century by century, miraculous feats of innovation, production, distribution, and social coordination. To the free market, we owe all material prosperity, all leisure time, our health and longevity, our huge and growing population and nearly everything we call life itself. Capitalism, and capitalism alone, has rescued the human race from degrading poverty, rampant sickness, and early death."

Lew Rockwell runs the Ludwig von Mises Institute in Auburn, Alabama. Over a recent weekend I read his excellent book, "Speaking of Liberty." He explains why so much hostility exists towards business. "Whether in the arts, entertainment, or academia, the dominant players are talented people who believe that they are wiser and better than the masses. They are appalled that capitalism permits a B-school dropout to become a billionaire while they scrape by for a measly raise when promoted from assistant to associate professor. They set out to cripple the system that brings this about."

And what does this envy lead to? Rockwell continues, "Outside of one or two economics professors, nearly the entire liberal arts faculty of the typical university is reliably anticapitalist. As a class, liberal arts academics can be depended on to oppose economic development, support high taxes, and latch on to every anti-enterprise cause that comes along."

Economist Thomas Sowell writes, "Think about the things that have improved our lives the most over the past century – medical advances, the transportation revolution, huge increases in consumer goods, dramatic improvements in housing, the computer revolution. The people who created these things – the doers – are not popular heroes. Our heroes are the talkers who complain about the doers."

He continues, "There was a time when most people lived and died within a 50-mile radius of where they were born. The automobile opened a whole new world to these people. It also enabled those living in overcrowded cities to spread out into suburbs and get some elbow room. Trucks got goods to people more cheaply and ambulances got people to hospitals to save their lives. Yet who among the people who did this are today regarded as being as big a hero as Ralph Nader, who put himself on the map with complaints about cars in general and the Corvair in particular? Hard data on automobile safety and tests conducted on the Corvair both undermined Nader's claims. But he will always be a hero to the talkers."

Lew Rockwell points out, "The philosopher who strolls around speculating on the meaning of life is seen as the highest form of humanity, while the man who risks his own money to make available food, shelter, medicine, clothing, and all the other material goods that make life livable is despised."

Animosity towards the merchant class has been around for centuries. Why? The goal of making a profit is quite obviously a self-serving motive. Other occupations, while equally self-serving, are better able to hide their motives. Even though a merchant must provide services for others in order to profit, that part of the equation is overlooked. They're condemned for making a profit.

Lew Rockwell explains how well this profit system works. "It balances human needs with the availability of all the world's resources, unleashes the amazing power of human creativity, and works to meet the material needs of every member of society at the least possible cost. It does this through exchange, cooperation, competition, entrepreneurship, and all the institutions that make possible capitalism – the most productive economic system this side of heaven."

Not long ago I read an article about China and the kind of heroes they glorify in their media. They write about entrepreneurs and business leaders. Contrast that with our hero worship of hip-hop musicians and dysfunctional movie stars. You can read newspaper and magazine articles endlessly about athletes, politicians and entertainers, but not business people (except for a handful, like Martha Stewart, who get into trouble). Do you have any doubts that the Asians will outdo us?

CHAPTER EIGHTEEN
THIS IS A RECORDING

"All government operation is wasteful, inefficient, and serves the bureaucrat rather than the consumer."
— Murray Rothbard

"Government control gives rise to fraud, suppression of the truth, intensification of the black market and artificial scarcity. Above all, it unmans the people and deprives them of initiative, it undoes the teaching of self-help."
— Gandhi

"The bureaucrat is not free to aim at improvement. He is bound to obey rules and regulations established by a superior body. He has no right to embark upon innovations if his superiors do not approve of them. His duty and his virtue is to be obedient."
— Ludwig von Mises

The other day I had reason to call a government agency. On the first dial I got a machine that gave me a choice of recorded options, none of which I wanted. I kept calling trying to get a human to answer. Finally, after much dialing I got the name of the person I needed. I called his number and got a recorded message that promised to call me if I left my number. That was a week ago and I still haven't heard back.

I shudder to think what happens when we turn more and more of our economy over to the government. Newly elected politicians always think they're the anointed ones that can make the government more effective and efficient. However, nobody can. That's because the government has no bottom line. Since they don't operate under a profit or loss system, they have no objective standard to measure results. Their yardstick for success is their own opinion. They often measure effectiveness by how much money they spend. Inevitably they lobby for more funding; there is no incentive for cost cutting or sound financial management among bureaucrats.

Government doesn't rely on merit the way business does. They tend to measure employees by credentials and educational degrees. Merit takes a back seat to not rocking the boat. Often the government hires and promotes people based on race and gender rather than ability and talent. Such policies can overlook the deserving and reward the incompetent. The work ethic suffers when a good effort and a poor effort are treated the same. Employees who can't cut it are rarely laid off or fired.

Bureaucratic management has more rules and regulations than does private business because the law imposes restrictions on arbitrary government authority. There is little room for flexibility or independent thinking. Common sense is sacrificed to follow the letter of the law. These rigid policies destroy innovation and creativity. Despite tremendous overkill in staffing at every level the government can't get out of its own way.

All too often political influence affects the quality of work that government does. Special interest groups and lobbyists tug the government in all directions at once. The bigger the government with all its regulations and hoops to jump through the greater the chance of corruption. Government always bites off more than it can chew. Instead of doing a good job on a few things it does a bad job at a lot of things.

We've all experienced the ineptitude of government. If you want to see the greatness of free markets and capitalism all you need to do is go to the mall. If you want to see the effectiveness of government all you need to do is pick up the phone and dial them. If you get a real person to answer please let me know how you did it.

(Most of these arguments were originally made in the excellent book, *Bureaucracy*, by Ludwig Von Mises.)

CHAPTER NINETEEN
REAPING THE WHIRLWIND

"Statism survives by looting; a free country survives by production."

– Ayn Rand

"The appearance of periodically recurring economic crises is the necessary consequence of repeatedly renewed attempts to reduce the 'natural' rates of interest on the market by means of banking policy."   – Ludwig von Mises

Several years ago I got a book in the mail from the late economist, Hans Sennholz. He was a professor of economics and a student of Ludwig von Mises while at NYU. The title, *Sowing the Wind*, is a play on the Old Testament passage, "For they have sown the wind, and they shall reap the whirlwind."

Professor Sennholz was an intrepid critic of government deficits. "If we cannot return to fiscal integrity because the public prefers profusion and prodigality over balanced budgets, we cannot escape paying the price, which is ever lower incomes and standards of living for all. The pains of economic stagnation and decline which are plaguing us today are likely to intensify and multiply in the coming years. The social and racial conflict, which springs from the redistribution ideology, may deepen as economic output is shrinking and transfer 'entitlements' cause budget deficits to soar. The U.S. dollar, which has become a mere corollary of government finance, is unlikely to survive the soaring deficits."

He explains how government deficits expand. "When the public demand for government services and benefits grows beyond the ability of business and wealthy taxpayers to pay, budgetary deficits become unavoidable. After all, the popularity of redistribution by political force tends to grow with every dollar of 'free' service rendered. The clamor finally becomes so intense that, in order to be heard, every new call is presented as an 'emergency' that must be met immediately before all others. Redistributive government then rushes from one emergency to another, trying to meet the most noise and politically potent demands."

On the subject of debt he writes, "The man who lives above his present circumstances is in great danger of soon living much beneath them. The same is true with a group of people called 'society.' To live beyond its means is to invite poverty and deprivation...deficit spending...consumes substance and wealth, engages in mass deceit about economic reality, sets a poor example to others, makes people dependent and subservient, causes uncertainty and instability, and breeds social conflict and strife. It may even weaken the political institutions of a free society."

He argues that the capital consumed by government would have been better spent in private hands. "It is difficult to estimate the number of factories and stores that were not built, the tools and dies that were not cast, the jobs not created, the wages not paid, the food, clothing and shelter not produced on account of this massive consumption of capital. The coming generation of Americans and countless others to come will be poorer by far as a result of our deficit spending.

"Of course, the beneficiaries of the redistribution process may enjoy every moment of it. With present-oriented people, today's enjoyment is always more pleasurable than saving for tomorrow. In their ignorance, they may applaud the very favors and handouts that are destroying their jobs and the wages they could have earned."

Mr. Sennholz explains the nasty consequences of America's financial bubbles. "Many failed to recognize the gradual development of financial bubbles especially in equity markets and real estate. Bubbles, which ultimately must deflate and come to naught, are difficult to spot because they closely resemble real economic expansion. They look like genuine capital formation which causes interest rates to decline, profits to rise, and asset prices to advance. Actually, they are visible symptoms of maladjustments caused by wanton money and credit creation and false interest rates. They enjoy the loud support and confirmation by the monetary authorities blowing the bubbles and by politicians who love the booms.

"While true economic expansion builds on genuine saving and capital formation, a financial bubble springs from deliberate money and credit creation which falsifies interest rates and goods prices, misleads businessmen and consumers, wastes productive capital, and benefits a few speculators at the expense of multitudes of investors."

Mr. Sennholz makes no bones about the final outcome. "The ultimate destination of the present road of political *fiat* is hyperinflation with all its ominous economic, social and political consequences. On this road, no federal plan, program, incomes policy, control, nationalization, threat, fine, or prison can prevent the continuous erosion and ultimate destruction of the dollar."

CHAPTER TWENTY
JOBS AND INFLATION

"Paper money always returns to its intrinsic value – zero."   – Voltaire

"Whether ancient or modern, monarchy or republic, coin or paper, each nation descends pretty much the same slippery slope, expanding government to address perceived needs, accumulating too much debt, and then repudiating its obligations by destroying its currency."   – James Turk and John Rubino

"To combat the depression by a forced credit expansion is to attempt to cure the evil by the very means which brought it about."   – Friedrich Hayek

Has there ever been a country that improved its economic health by monetizing its debt? As far as I can tell any country that regularly created money to ~~ y its bills suffered greatly from inflation and economic deterioration. Any country that has done what the U.S. is doing now, not only wrecked the value of its currency, it brought hardship to its citizenry. These periodic episodes of raw inflating are among the worst thing a country can do to itself. Apparently the lessons of history don't count with our monetary authorities.

Another question is whether increasing taxes has ever caused an economy to improve. Have tax increases ever added to the prosperity of a country? I can't find an example in the history of the world where higher taxes improved the lot of the people. In fact, it appears to be just the opposite. The greater the tax burden the less economic progress.

When a company makes a profit they hire more people. When government takes a big share of those profits it means less expansion for the company and fewer new hires. By taking a company's profits under the guise of creating jobs the government kills jobs. Ludwig von Mises wrote, "Government spending cannot create additional jobs. If the government provides the funds required by taxing the citizens or borrowing from the public, it abolishes on the one hand as many jobs as it creates on the other."

The final question is whether a combination of high taxes and persistent money creation have ever made a country more prosperous? The answer is never. They have only made countries poorer. They have caused social unrest, injustice and poverty. These practices have only torn countries apart. They are in the process of doing the same thing to America. Of taxes Mises said, "Confiscatory taxation results in declining progress and...brings about a general trend towards stagnation..." Of inflation he said, "Only apparent and temporary relief can be won by tricks of banking and currency. In the long run they must land the nation in a profounder catastrophe."

Are we headed towards catastrophe? Author Mark Steyn answers, "In the Western world, countries that were once the crucible of freedom are slipping remorselessly into a thinly disguised serfdom in which an ever higher proportion of your assets are annexed by the state as superlandlord. Big government is where nations go to die – not in Keynes' 'long run,' but sooner than you think."

CHAPTER TWENTY-ONE
WASHINGTON WEALTH

"'Need' now means wanting someone else's money. 'Greed' means wanting to keep your own. 'Compassion' is when a politician arranges the transfer."

– Joseph Sobran

"No longer are Republicans arguing with Democrats about whether government should be big or small. Instead they are at odds over what kind of big government the U.S. should have."

– Janet Hook

A recent online article from *Forbes* listed the wealthiest 24 counties in America. Not surprisingly 12 of the 24 were in Virginia and Maryland clustered around Washington D.C. When almost half of all earnings and profits are delivered to Washington to be passed out to favorite constituencies a lot of it greases the locals. Consulting firms, sub-contractors and others are funded first for so-called equitable outcomes and then for the job to be done.

Furthermore, every big corporation or interest group has to open an office or hire a lawyer or lobbyist to secure specials favors or to keep the government from ruining them. Then you have a growing army of government workers. A federal employee now earns about twice what private sector employees get. Currently there's an increase in U.S. government employees while private employers are cutting jobs. Then there are the fat retirement benefits for government workers, many who retire at age 50.

The Heritage Foundation recently reported, "The Washington economy is booming as private firms have been forced to hire legions of lawyers and lobbyists to both protect their firms from Obama's new agenda and find ways they can turn it into profit. This is why energy companies are spending millions on lobbyists to shape legislation instead of on scientists to find energy. It is why software companies are spending millions on lawyers to get federal government business instead of on engineers to develop new technologies."

Back in 1994, columnist Jonathan Rauch explains what happens when Washington becomes a center of profit for the private sector: "Economic thinkers have recognized for generations that every person has two ways to become wealthier. One is to produce more, the other is to capture more of what others produce...Washington looks increasingly like a public works jobs program for lawyers and lobbyists, a profit center for professionals who are in business for themselves."

CHAPTER TWENTY-THREE
LIBERAL TRANSFORMATION

"The fact is that the New Deal was, overall, a dismal failure."　　– Mark R. Levin

"Vast numbers of Americans today look to Washington for a rich array of 'entitlements' that speak of nothing so much as the illusion of something for nothing."
– Roger Pilon

"Once Congress establishes that one person can live at the expense of another, it pays for everyone to try to do so."　　– Walter Williams

Years ago I sold insurance for a living. In my office hung a picture of President Lyndon Johnson. Because of his "Great Society" initiative that helped the poor, I thought he was the greatest President ever. I had come to be a liberal by reading the popular literature of the day. This included economist John Kenneth Galbraith, and most especially, the philosopher Bertrand Russell, an ardent pacifist and socialist. I also subscribed to the *I.F. Stone Weekly*, a leftist newsletter.

When I was a kid, my father was transferred to St. Louis, Missouri. At the time, the government was planning a massive housing project in St. Louis for the poor called Pruit-Igo. In the 1950s these huge high rises were built and occupied. In 1961 I was stationed at an Air Force base near St. Louis. I got to see these subsidized housing projects once again. They looked unkempt. Ten years later, by 1970, they were run down and nearly uninhabitable. Each building became a behavioral sinkhole. Crime, drugs, prostitution, child abuse, poverty and illegitimacy ran out of control. The government had to demolish the huge and expensive buildings. Liberals claimed they failed because they were too big. If only the government would build smaller units they argued, all would be well.

In 1971 I became friends with Bernard T. Daley of Minneapolis. For a while he was my business partner. Bernard was a brilliant Irishman who loved to discuss politics. His primary mission in life was converting liberals and middle-of-the-roaders to a libertarian viewpoint. He was heavily influenced by the freedom philosopher Leonard Read, who believed that by improving yourself and your knowledge you would become a beacon for others. Bernie Daley certainly was that. Unfortunately, he died in 1982 at the young age of

48. To this day I know many of his friends and associates who were once liberals. They continue to believe and promote the libertarian, conservative, free market case.

Within months of meeting Bernie he began to overturn my liberal views. He invariably pointed to the failure and sorry results of government social programs. Prior to meeting Bernie I'd never thought much about the reason Pruit-Igo in St. Louis had failed so miserably. Now I concluded that welfare and subsidies made matters worse. Bernie was always asking me to analyze the results of government initiatives. Once I began to do that, my thinking changed.

I did something that most liberals never do. I examined the consequences of the programs I once so ardently championed. It's easier for a Muslim to swear off Mohamed than for a liberal to see that giving people money they didn't earn harms them. That's why we hear so much socialist rot from the candidates who want to help the middle class, help the poor and help everyone else who has a problem or made a mess out of their life. It's the same weak-kneed response coming from the current administration now sending everyone free money. They are turning America into a nation of moochers. It's time that someone told Americans to stand on their own two feet and take their lumps in life without whining or expecting a free ride. Life is about struggle and you don't get anywhere without it. It's long past time for everyone to try a little rugged individualism. America didn't become a great nation through government assistance.

CHAPTER TWENTY-FOUR
BECOMING LENIN

"If the Liberal Left can create the common perception that success and failure are simple matters of 'fortune' or 'luck,' then it is easy to promote and justify their various income redistribution schemes."
— Neal Boortz

"A private-property, market system has much to recommend it. A system is more moral if it holds individuals accountable for their actions and encourages them to help others than if it allows them to impose costs on others without their consent."
— Peter Hill

There's a generally held belief that an upward limit exists on how high taxes can be raised. If taxes go too much higher, there's no question it would damage the economy. However, that will not persuade the left wing or their political candidates to forego tax increases. Liberals refuse to see that high taxes hurt progress. They listen to left-leaning economic propaganda that ignores the evidence and claims that higher taxes will make little or no difference.

For the most part they don't care about economic consequences as long as their precious social programs get funded. And, if some rich folks get the shaft, it's all the more fun. There's a deep vein of envy on the left. It wouldn't bother them a bit to see taxes on the wealthy go to 90% with strict limits on what people can earn and what they can own. They are currently advocating excess profits taxes, raising the income tax, hiking the capital gains tax, increasing state income taxes, sales taxes and corporate taxes.

What's truly frightening is how close liberals are to winning elections and controlling political outcomes. Once they get into power, social costs will rise precipitously and taxes will become punitive. Most leftists would secretly like to become Lenin. Since they share his view that wealth and success are only a matter of luck, it wouldn't bother them to strip the affluent of every penny.

If enough people rely on the government for their financial survival, it going to happen and it's closer than you think. Author James Bovard reminds us, "Government aid programs have been endlessly expanded, and the government has sought to maximize the number of people willing to accept handouts...Roughly half of all Americans are dependent on the government, either for handouts, pensions, or paychecks...There are more than 20 million government employees in the United States – more than the total number of Americans employed in manufacturing...The sheer number of government employees and welfare recipients effectively transforms the purpose of government from maintaining order to confiscating as much as possible from vulnerable taxpayers...Once a person becomes a government dependent, his moral standing to resist the expansion of government power is fatally compromised."

There's a lot at stake in these elections. If the redistributors and their subsidized followers win out, America's waning greatness will fade away for good. The downside is a nightmare. It's the road to hyperinflation, depression, dollar destruction, national decline and insolvency. Ludwig von Mises instructed, "No one can find a safe way out for himself if society is sweeping towards destruction. Therefore everyone, in his own interests, must thrust himself vigorously into the intellectual battle. None can stand aside with unconcern; the interests of everyone hang on the result. Whether he chooses or not, every man is drawn into the great historical struggle, the decisive battle into which our epoch has plunged us."

CHAPTER TWENTY-FIVE
THE PAPER CHASE

"The effect of capitalism is to steer human selfishness so that, through the invisible hand of competition, the energies of the capitalist produce the abundance from which the whole society benefits."
— Dinesh D'Souza

"Instead of promoting a rational society of competent adults who solve the problems of living through voluntary cooperation, the modern liberal agenda creates an irrational society of child-like adults who depend upon governments to take care of them."
— Lyle H. Rossiter, Jr.

Once upon a time immigrants to America had a hard row to hoe. The land of opportunity offered only that. If you worked hard, you could make a decent life for yourself. America became a land of "rugged individualists." In those days, Americans asked for nothing more than freedom and the chance to strive for a better life.

There was no subsidized housing, no food stamps or other benefits to make life easier. When you got sick, the government didn't pay your doctor bill. That's all changed. Most of today's immigrants get subsidies of one sort or another. Naturally, if you get food stamps and free housing, that's an incentive to come here.

My mother was born in Buffalo, New York. She traced her lineage back to colonial times. When she was a young girl, her widowed father was transferred by his company to Canada. There she met my dad. After I was born they decided to try and emigrate to the U.S. They went through a lot of paperwork and finally got us admitted.

My father was coming to the U.S. to take a job in the insurance business. No subsidies of any kind awaited. In fact, there was a stigma attached to any kind of government handout. At that time, welfare was doled out to a small segment of the populace and they were looked down on. A black mark was attached to welfare or unemployment compensation, and nobody with any gumption would consider these options.

In 50 years, all of that has changed. An army of the entitled (the government's term) works the system for maximum benefit. The politicians bend over to give them more freebies. The subsidized even have their own lobbyists to make sure the handouts keep coming. The line at the government trough grows longer by the day, as new programs give away more and more.

In order to pay for this spend-fest, the government has to print money to cover its deficits. This inflation of the purchasing media is a necessary requisite to fund the numerous socialist schemes that have overtaken the land of rugged individualists. This watering down of the currency pays for the subsidies that have rendered so many people dependent, dishonest and helpless. It's a social mess that only the government could engineer.

Whenever I write about the social schemes that are breaking the budget, I get angry e-mails and letters from people who say I'm forgetting the cost of war. Yes, inflationary purchasing media also pays for the war. That's why the Libertarians call it the welfare-warfare state. Whatever the reason for these vast expenditures, the currency is being debased. You can't have socialism and foreign adventures with a sound currency. You have to have printing press money and credit inflation to pay for it.

Now the credit binge initiated by the U.S. has spread globally. Everybody's doing it. As Richard Russell points out, "The world fiat money situation has existed for only 35 years, and already under the care of the world's central banks, it's out of control – or as a teenager might express it, its 'money gone wild.'"

Years ago the economic thinker and author, Henry Hazlitt, warned, "Once the idea is accepted that money is something whose supply is determined simply by the printing press, it becomes impossible for the politicians in power to resist the constant demand for further inflation...If the welfarist-socialist-inflationist-trend of recent years continues in this country, the outlook is dark."

CHAPTER TWENTY-SIX
SLIPPERY SLOPE

"The friendliness and charity of our countrymen can always be relied upon to relieve their fellow citizens in misfortune. This has been repeatedly and quite lately demonstrated. Federal aid in such cases encourages the expectation of paternal care on the part of the Government and weakens the sturdiness of our national character, while it prevents the indulgence among our people of that kindly sentiment and conduct which strengthens the bonds of a common brotherhood."

– Grover Cleveland

"If you put the federal government in charge of the Sahara Desert, in 5 years there'd be a shortage of sand."
– Milton Friedman

"He is base – and that is the one base thing in the universe – to receive favors and render none."
– Ralph Waldo Emerson

They have intensive care units in hospitals now specifically for newborn babies that are having problems. It's expensive. I know, because my new granddaughter spent three days there. It was over $30,000. There was another baby there born premature. He was a crack baby and weighed only two pounds. The nurse said he'd be there up to five months.

Later I thought about the bill for this tiny infant struggling for life. It would cost about $1,200,000 and the state would have to pay it. Then I thought some more about the kind of life he would have. With a drug-addicted mother, there was little chance he would get the love and nurturing necessary to be a well-adjusted and productive person. More likely he would be in trouble with the law and have his own problems with drugs and alcohol.

No doubt his mother would continue to rely on the government to pay for raising him. She would get aid for her dependent children, public housing, health care and food stamps. When you add all the assistance up, it would probably run close to $25,000 a year for him. That would go on for twenty years or so until he began to get assistance directly. Then he would get the same benefits his mother received including subsidized rent and a welfare check. If he wanted to claim that he suffered from depression, he could get another $1,000 a month from Social Security. Should he take the time to file a tax return, he could get another welfare payment at tax time. Chances are he'd be in and out of the court system. That's also costly. He would need a public defender, court time, incarceration, a parole officer, and the continued attention of the police. As an adult he would probably require at least $50,000 a year in social expenditures. Should he live to age 70, that's a total of $4,200,000 in social costs for him. These are rough estimates, but you get the picture.

There are millions of dependent people in similar circumstances in America. Their numbers are growing dramatically. What you subsidize you get more of. In addition, the U.S. government imports poor immigrants, some of whom begin to rely on social programs permanently. Once these expensive programs are in place they are almost impossible to stop. They change the culture. Look at the difference in how we handle old folks from just five or six decades ago. There's no way to go back. Social programs are a slippery slope. Once they take root they grow until they are unaffordable and irreversible. Eventually their runaway costs ruin a nation.

When social costs become too expensive, the voters will put left-wing politicians into power who promise to keep the free money coming. The high taxes they force on us will deprive the private sector of capital and incentives. The economy will weaken further and the government will be forced to increase social spending all the more. It will be a mess as only the government can create.

There is something else even more important. When you give money to people that they didn't earn, it weakens their character. Horrible things happen to little children every day in our country, and it was not always so. We rarely read about the epidemic of addiction that afflicts the underclass. The liberal media doesn't like to mention it. In fact, it's become the liberal blind spot.

A while ago I wrote a letter to Anna Quindlan, a *Newsweek* columnist, pointing this out. She had mentioned the positive charity work of the nuns. "How nicely you put it," I wrote. "'Touch the sick, the poor, the children, the powerless...' However, what you liberals forget is that you've taken charity out of private hands and turned it over to the government. That has engineered a social disaster. How many hundreds of blocks in your city or mine are you afraid to walk through on a summer evening? Giving people money that they didn't earn is the worst thing you can do to them. You have a blind spot about the sorry consequences of your social sympathy. You liberals refuse to see the horror and the magnitude of it because of your complicity."

The consequences of social welfare need to be recognized as America's greatest problem. Each day thousands of new infants are born who have no chance of being normal or productive. Their parents doom them from the start. Financial and economic problems can somehow be overcome. Social problems of the kind we have in America cannot be overcome. When a small child is ruined, they are generally ruined for life. Nobody's addressing these problems. Government just keeps getting bigger, always spending more to keep the welfare advocates appeased. In time we will be swept into the vortex of a financial crisis brought on by the government's deficits and the inflationary effect of the money created to pay the tab.

CHAPTER TWENTY-SEVEN
ENVY

"The cheap but simple human emotion of envy is the driving force of all social-ism, of all anti-capitalist philosophy. It is the mark of the intellectual."
– Andrew J. Galambos

"Rule by the statist elite is not benign or simply a matter of who happens to be in office: it is rule by a growing army of leeches and parasites fattening off the income and wealth of hard-working Americans, destroying their property, cor-rupting their customs and institutions, sneering at their religion."
– Murray Rothbard

"Social justice rests on the hate towards those that enjoy a comfortable posi-tion, namely, upon envy."
– Friedrich Hayek

I have these two acquaintances who are big believers in high taxes and heavy government regulation. One is a lawyer who did OK in his career but never made a lot of money. The other was in real estate and after years of disap-pointing results retired with modest means. They are both envious of people who made a lot of money. Envy is what makes them liberals.

Scratch a leftist and you'll find a person who's worried about someone else making a profit or high income. Why is that? Envy explains these sentiments. Author Helmut Schoek writes, "Envy is a drive which lies at the core of man's life as a social being..." In America the politics of envy can get you elected to the highest office in the land.

Under capitalism, everyone has the opportunity to become an entrepreneur or attain a profession or position that pays off handsomely. However, this sys-tem allows no excuses for personal shortcomings or failures. Most self-made people started from the same place as others who failed or who did not forge ahead. The sight of people who have given proof of greater ability bothers some people. To console themselves they rationalize that their skills have gone unrecognized. They blame capitalism, which they claim does not reward the meritorious but gives the prize to dishonest businesses, and other exploiters. They were too honest to swindle people, and they chose virtue over riches.

In a society where everyone is the founder of his or her own fortune, it is par-ticularly galling to the teacher, the politician, the artist or the bureaucrat to see the large income disparity between themselves and successful entrepreneurs. Their envy turns them to socialism, which promises to level incomes and allows the state to control economic outcomes.

The Austrian economist Ludwig von Mises put it this way, "Envy is a widespread frailty. It is certain that many intellectuals envy the higher income of prosperous businessmen and that these feelings drive them toward socialism. They believe that the authorities of a socialist commonwealth would pay them higher salaries than those that they earn under capitalism."

Mises further argued, "What pushes the masses into the camp of socialism is even more than the illusion that socialism will make them richer, the expectation that it will curb all those who are better than they themselves are..."

Even among some conservatives there exists an unhealthy level of envy toward the wealthy. They join with professors and politicians to suggest that the worst exploitation and greed comes from big business. They fail to realize that large corporations got that way because they did a superior job of meeting the product needs of the people in the best, most economical way.

The hallmark of big business is mass production for the benefit of the masses. In fact, big business standardizes the people's ways of consumption and enjoyment, and every citizen shares in most of these material blessings.

As for Wall Street, the current fiasco exemplifies pigging out at the government banquet table. When the government grants subsidies or provides cheap loans abuses are inevitable. When the government guarantees financial assets and removes risk, excesses are bound to occur. When the government keeps interest rates artificially low and money and credit loose speculators and risk takers push the envelope. When the regulators fail as they usually do, abuses occur and tremendous losses are inflicted on gullible investors who think that regulation protects them. When the government incentivizes social goals such as low income housing by throwing out the rulebook plenty of people will jump on the bandwagon. People are always going to take the most for themselves if it's available. Furthermore, the excesses of Wall Street hardly personify the vast number of businesses that are truly representative of capitalism.

Nobody goes without in the market economy because someone got rich. The same process that makes people rich satisfies people's wants and needs. The most millionaires are found in countries with the highest living standards. The entrepreneurs and the capitalists prosper only to the extent that they succeed in supplying and satisfying the consumer.

The glaring misunderstanding of capitalism and how it works in our society originates more from envy than intellect. This mix of envy and ignorance explains everything from the inroads of Lenin to the socialists who have led us down the path to fewer freedoms and more government. The liberals in our government promote a detrimental socialist philosophy. While Asia moves towards capitalism and prosperity, we are stuck with more big government.

CHAPTER TWENTY-EIGHT
SOCIAL WEAKENING

"Capitalism offers nothing but frustrations and rebuff to those who wish – because of claimed superiority of intelligence, birth, credentials, or ideals – to get without giving, to take without risking, to profit without sacrifice, to be exalted without humbling themselves to understand others and meet their needs."

– George Gilder

"Government sponsors untold waste, criminality and inequality in every sphere of life it touches, giving little or nothing in return." – Doug Casey

Our daily newspaper ran several articles about alcoholism and crime at one of Minnesota's Indian reservations. Teenage boys and girls had been thrown in jail for drunkenness as many as fifteen times. There had been a brutal murder. I wrote the following letter to the editor about this problem.

"After one hundred years of subsidies native Americans are worse off. When is the left going to figure out that giving money to people that they didn't earn is destructive to them? Liberals have done more harm than good with their runaway social sympathy. It's time to acknowledge this failure.

"Instead you run an editorial that suggests the cure is to 'listen to the elders.' Do you expect us to take such sentimental fluff seriously? Stop the government money and let people sink or swim. That's the cure, and the only cure, no matter how you deny it or search for another answer."

My letter didn't get published, so I e-mailed the following. "My letter on Leech Lake presented a viewpoint that was not covered by any of the other articles or opinions. Furthermore, it's crucial to understanding the behavioral disaster on the reservations.

"Solicitations I receive from native American charities claim a 90% alcoholism rate on Minnesota reservations, yet your lead Sunday editorial suggests that reservation problems can somehow be solved by 'listening to the elders.'

"You served up this bizarre opinion and nobody got to counter it. I believe my letter didn't get published because of your editor's liberal bias. Either that or your editor is inept in presenting all sides of an issue. Please note that I tried a second time. I believe my letter rankled liberal sentiments and was therefore rejected."

The whole matter caused me to think a lot about why liberals can't seem to see the obvious. We've been giving billions of dollars to millions of people for decades. Anyone can see they are worse off for it. The number of people living on government subsidies continues to escalate. Bad behavior has become an epidemic. Without any requirement to work people begin to get bored. Too often, they turn to wrongdoing for stimulation.

In 1946, the U.S. began to send monthly checks to inhabitants of an island in the Pacific that was next to an atomic bomb testing site. These self-sufficient islanders fished as a way of life. "Sixty Minutes" did a segment on these people after forty years of living on the dole. Since they had no need to fish anymore, many had forgotten how to fish. With no requirement to do anything, their alcohol consumption skyrocketed and social problems set in. Piles of beer cans and other junk marred the island's appearance.

Nothing damages people more than giving them money they didn't earn. We have evolved through hardship. Economic challenges and financial struggles make us what we are. Remove the demand to make our own way and behavior deteriorates.

It's hardly an original thought. They've been writing about it for centuries. "An idle man's brain is the devil's workshop," wrote Bunyan. "I look at indolence as a sort of suicide," wrote Chesterfield. Beecher said, "If you are idle you are on the road to ruin, and there are few stopping places upon it. It is rather a precipice than a road." Emerson wrote, "He is base – and that is the one base thing in the universe – to receive favors and render none." Proverbs express the absolute wisdom of the ages. "Idleness rusts the mind." "To do nothing teaches to do ill." "Industry is the parent of virtue." "Idleness is the root of all evil." "He becometh poor that dealeth with a slack hand." "It is a great weariness to do nothing."

Two hundred and fifty years ago the religious thinker Swedenborg described a process which goes on today in subsidizing the worst elements of society. "It is believed by many that love to the neighbour consists in giving to the poor, in assisting the needy, and in doing good to everyone; but charity consists in acting prudently, and to the end that good may result. He who assists a poor or needy villain does evil to his neighbour through him; for through the assistance which he renders he confirms him in evil, and supplies him with the means of doing evil to others."

Every day incalculable numbers of children in our country are sexually and physically abused. They witness violence, mayhem and depravity. They hear vile language and often they go unsupervised, free to use drugs and keep the hours they choose. Their parents are totally unfit for child raising, yet they are subsidized all the more. Twenty-five million children live in homes without fathers. Two million have parents in prison. How is it that a problem of this magnitude, surely the greatest problem facing any nation, could be such a neglected topic?

In order to confront this behavioral disaster, the left would have to admit responsibility for engineering social programs that have gone astray. After all, it is their social sympathy and their politics that engineered the government schemes that weakened so many people. The policies they support are the cause of much of the misery they are so compassionate about. They meant to do good, but they did harm. It's not easy for them to admit that their epic social blunder has ruined the character of so many people.

Because the left will refuse to see their mistake, they will continue to resist any kind of solution. So there is little or no hope that anything will change. We will continue to take increasing amounts of money from those who earned it and give it to increasing numbers of those who didn't. Today both parties enthusiastically ladle out billions in subsidies. Unfortunately, the recipients will be all the worse for it. Does anybody seriously think this is going to have a good ending?

CHAPTER TWENTY-NINE
A MYTHICAL INTERVIEW WITH
LUDWIG VON MISES

"A nation that encourages its people to spend more and save less promotes economic backwardness, social decay and its own financial doom."

– Kurt Richebacher

"It is all too easy for the liberal media to stir up the irrational hatreds of millions of people, who see themselves as less fortunate than others, by repeatedly talking about the billions of dollars in 'windfall profits' earned by major corporations, by featuring periodic stories on the opulent living of wealthy individuals, or by pointing an accusing finger at 'loopholes' used by 'the rich.'"

– Robert Ringer

"No government can provide social security. It is not in the nature of government to be able to provide anything. Government itself is not self-supporting. It lives by taxation. Therefore, since it cannot provide for itself but by taking toll of what the people produce, how can it provide social security for the people?"

– Garet Garrett

Ludwig von Mises was the most influential economist in what is known as the Austrian School. He advocated limited government, free markets and sound money. In 1920 he proved that Communism and socialist planning must fail because of the absence of market pricing. He was credited with numerous other brilliant and important theoretical accomplishments.

His predictions and warnings have proven accurate. His followers have been the only effective forecasters of the current economic crisis. Austrian economics provides a financial compass for you. It stands in stark contrast to the failed Keynesian economics of Washington and Wall Street. It's imperative that you grasp the content of this interview and begin to think in terms of Austrian economics. Nothing I can tell you is more important.

The answers to the following questions are exact quotes from various books.

> Q. Over the past few decades our national savings rate has plummeted. What do you make of that?

A. Saving and the resulting accumulation of capital goods are at the beginning of every attempt to improve the material conditions of man; they are the foundation of human civilization.

Q. Please elaborate.

A. Saving, capital accumulation, and investment withhold the amount concerned from current consumption and dedicate it to the improvement of future conditions.

Q. Why have our national savings collapsed?

A. The policies advocated by the welfare school remove the incentive to saving on the part of private citizens.

Q. How important is the reversal of this trend?

A. If people do not consume their whole incomes, the non-consumed surplus can be invested, it increases the amount of capital goods available and thereby makes it possible to embark upon projects which could not be executed before.

Q. How does the Keynesian economics practiced in Washington impact this view?

A. The essence of Keynesianism is its complete failure to conceive the role that saving and capital accumulation play in the improvement of economic conditions.

Q. Why isn't this more widely understood?

A. Most people take it simply for granted that some mysterious factor is operative that makes the nation richer from year to year.

Q. What do you say to them?

A. Do the American voters know that the unprecedented improvement in their standard of living that the last hundred years brought was the result of the steady rise in the per-head quota of capital invested? Do they realize that every measure leading to capital decumulation jeopardizes their prosperity?

Q. Are you saying that capital is scarce?

A. Strictly speaking, capital has always been scarce and will always be. The available supply of capital goods can never become so abundant that all projects, the execution of which could improve the material well-being of people, could be undertaken. If it were otherwise, mankind would live in the Garden of Eden and would not have to bother at all about production.

Q. How does this impact us today?

A. A nation cannot prosper if its members are not fully aware of the fact that what alone can improve their conditions is more and better production. And this can only be brought about by increased saving and capital accumulation.

Q. How do you explain the influence of Keynes on contemporary politics?

A. The unprecedented success of Keynesianism is due to the fact that it provides an apparent justification for the 'deficit spending' policies of contemporary governments. It is the pseudo-philosophy of those who can think of nothing else than to dissipate the capital accumulated by previous generations.

Q. You mean inflating?

A. Yes, deficit spending means increasing the quantity of money in circulation. That the official terminology avoids calling it inflation is of no avail whatever.

Q. Inflating is more popular than ever.

A. Inflationism is the oldest of all fallacies.

Q. What's the main argument against it?

A. Credit expansion and inflationary increases of the quantity of money frustrate the 'common man's' attempts to save and to accumulate reserves for less propitious days.

Q. Why is it so popular?

A. For the naïve mind there is something miraculous in the issuance of fiat money. A magic word spoken by the government creates out of nothing a thing which can be exchanged against any merchandise a man would like to get. How pale is the art of sorcerers, witches, and conjurors when compared with that of the government's Treasury Department.

Q. What are the consequences for the economy?

A. An artificial boom, a boom built entirely upon the illusions of ample and easy money.

Q. We've had that. What's next?

A. The inevitable result of inflationary policies is a drop in the monetary unit's purchasing power.

Q. The monetary authorities seem to think that's helpful.

A. Only the naïve inflationists could believe that government could enrich mankind through fiat money.

Q. There's no benefit?

A. No increase in the welfare of the members of a society can result from the availability of an additional quantity of money.

Q. What are some of the consequences?

A. Under the illusions created by the credit expansion, business has embarked upon projects for the execution of which the real savings are not rich enough. When this mal-investment becomes visible, the boom collapses.

Q. The economy worsens?

A. Credit expansion is not a nostrum to make people happy. The boom it engenders must inevitably lead to a debacle and unhappiness.

Q. Their answer is to lower interest rates. What do you say to this?

A. If one wants to avert depressions, one must abstain from any tampering with the rate of interest.

Q. Isn't it too late?

A. People must learn that the only means to avoid the recurrence of economic catastrophes is to let the market – and not the government – determine interest rates.

Q. We've ignored this lesson. What happens now?

A. The monetary and credit policies of all nations are headed for a new catastrophe, probably more disastrous than any of the older slumps.

Q. We are told that government spending will bail us out. What say you?

A. What the government spends is entirely taken from the pockets of the individual citizens and corporations. The spending and investing capacity of the public is curtailed to the same extent to which the spending ability of the government expands.

Q. Our current policies are for more of the same. What's your prognosis?

A. It has often been suggested to 'stimulate' economic activity and to 'prime the pump' by recourse to a new extension of credit which would allow the depression to be ended and bring about a recovery or at least a return to normal conditions; the advocates of this method forget, however, that even though it might overcome the difficulties of the moment, it will certainly produce a worse situation in a not too distant future.

Q. Aren't you afraid of a depression?

A. The depression is the process of liquidating the errors committed in the excesses of the artificial boom; it is the return to calm reasoning and a reasonable conduct of affairs within the limits of the available supply of capital goods. It is a painful process, but it is a process of restoration of business health.

Q. That will not happen. What's next for us?

A. If the credit expansion is not stopped in time, the boom turns into the crack-up boom; the flight into real values begins, and the whole monetary system founders.

CHAPTER THIRTY
THE LIBERAL LEGACY OF CRIME

"The army of relief and other subsidy recipients will continue to grow, and the solvency of the government will become increasingly untenable, as long as part of the population can vote to force the other part to support it." – Henry Hazlitt

"You cannot strengthen the weak by weakening the strong. You cannot help the wage earner by pulling down the wage payer. You cannot help the poor by destroying the rich. You cannot help men permanently by doing for then when they could and should do for themselves." – Abraham Lincoln

Is there anything worse that can befall a country than a financial catastrophe and depression? Yes, and it's happening right now. At least 100,000 new criminal predators are coming on to our streets this year. These juvenile delinquents under 20 years are in an age group known to be more violent and vicious than any other. For the most part, they originate within the underclass and are comprised of all races. Statistics are cloudy, but the number of them committing crimes could actually be as high as 250,000 and, worst of all, this is a trend that will continue to grow. In addition, six million people who served time in prison are out on the street, and over half of them are going back to jail. Meanwhile, our penitentiaries are stuffed full with one and a half million inmates.

Many of the underclass never get into trouble with the law themselves, but their dysfunctional behavior gets passed on to the next generation who may then resort to crime. We're not talking about some small slice of the population here, we're talking about a large, growing problem with which no modern nation has ever had to cope. Already, 32% of young black males will be incarcerated at least once. By some estimates, as many as 40% of the male population in the inner city will be ensnared in the criminal justice system. Unemployment in our central cities runs to 60% or higher. That's because normal employment opportunities are rejected, while illegal activities in the underground economy flourish.

Crime statistics indicate that children of single parents turn to delinquency at a higher rate. That makes it all the more worrisome that the percentage of children born out of wedlock among the underclass has reached levels that are beyond disgraceful. According to author, Mona Charen, "In 1960, the white rate of illegitimacy was 2 percent. In 1999, the rate was 27 percent. Among blacks, the 1960 rate was 23 percent. By 1999, it had climbed to near 70 percent. In some black neighborhoods, children can grow up without knowing anyone who is married." Read that last sentence again and ask yourself what kind of behavioral nightmare are these social programs creating? Mona Charen points out the reason. "Liberals...provided young women with the wherewithal (their own apartments and a monthly stipend) to make getting along without a husband possible, and to immature eyes, even desirable."

Unfortunately, the underclass has a birth rate approximately three times higher than the general populace. Project those growth rates a few decades into the future and you should be terrified as to what kind of dangerous society your grandchildren will inherit. When a half million vicious teenage hoodlums hit the streets every year, the cities will be worse than war zones. But don't expect the liberals, whose social programs created this mess, to see the error of their ways. They only know one cure for the various problems their programs create; more money, which only compounds the problem.

Liberals are great for broadcasting improvement in any small aspect of the crime rate. They downplay crime and mislead us on crime statistics. The day will come when murder doesn't make the newspapers. That's because liberals suspect there might be linkage between giving people money they didn't earn and their behavior. Hello! Liberals don't want to take the blame for a behavioral disaster of this magnitude, but they are responsible. I'll say it again, the liberal agenda is the blueprint for national ruin and socialism is the road to hell on earth. Our nation is traveling down that road.

CHAPTER THIRTY-ONE
CONSEQUENCES

"Every liberal initiative, from welfare to antismoking measures, is justified by reference to 'the children.' Yet the clear result of liberal policies is to harm children even more than adults."
— Mona Charen

"Recipients of transfers tend to become less self-reliant and more dependent on government payments. When people can get support without exercising their own abilities to discover and respond to opportunities for earning income, those abilities atrophy. People forget – or never learn in the first place – how to help themselves, and eventually some of them simply accept their helplessness."
— Robert Higgs

I had a few hours to kill last Sunday before a flock of grandkids showed up to open Christmas presents. Since I was caught up on my reading I clicked on the TV and channel surfed until I came across the 1965 movie, Dr. Zhivago, which was just starting. The part I remembered and wanted to see again came about half way through the movie. The doctor, played by Omar Sharif, had returned to Moscow after two years at the front in World War I. The Bolsheviks were now firmly entrenched, running the country.

Zhivago had married into a wealthy family before the war and when he returned to their large and once lovely household he was in for a shock. A couple of dozen shabbily dressed party members had taken over the house. He and his family were relegated to one bedroom. Any complaints about their misfortune would be cause for arrest. They acquiesced to this theft of their property out of fear.

Frankly, the difference between the Russian Bolsheviks and today's leftists in American isn't that great. They differ only by a matter of degree. The Communists in Russia got everything you owned. So far the liberals have only been successful in getting half of what you earn, plus half of what you own when you die. Philosophically, the liberals, the Marxists and the socialists are blood brothers. They all wish to address social injustice, raise taxes, put the government in control of the economy and redistribute the wealth of the nation through subsidies. Their heightened sense of social sympathy makes them antagonistic to the accomplishments of capitalism. Their outrage over the inequality of incomes overrides any concern for the dire economic consequences of their policies.

What the liberals stand for has always failed when put into practice. It is failing now before our eyes. It will always fail. These leftist schemes promise national ruin. That the historical failure of collectivism is not properly acknowledged by the left speaks of their myopic stubbornness.

Once you commit the first dollar to a government social program it's the beginning of the end. The number of these programs never stops expanding. At first there was one, now there are thousands. Furthermore, the existing programs never stop growing and costs rise relentlessly. You have a three-headed monster; new programs, growth of existing programs and runaway costs of all programs. When the government can't pay for them they borrow or print new money to keep them funded. This debases our currency, acts as a hidden tax and spreads a contagion of ills associated with inflation. It's how nations go bankrupt.

That's not the worst of it. Government social programs don't work. None of them accomplish what they set out to do. In fact, they make matters worse. We've spent hundreds of billions to eradicate poverty. Yet the economic and social condition of welfare recipients is much worse than when these programs started. Despite public housing, rent subsidies, food stamps, welfare payments and more, the long-term recipients of entitlements have essentially become a hoard of drug addicts and alcoholics. Bad character has triumphed.

Worst of all, the attitudes of the underclass and their sympathizers have turned into a frightful animosity towards the prevailing culture. The more money they get the louder their accusations of racism, inequality and injustice. The more they are subsidized, the more they express hatred for America, curse capitalism and support a radical agenda. They make up false charges to justify their shakedown of America. Their leadership gains money and power while encouraging a belief in victimhood.

Whatever you subsidize, you get more of. That's why the numbers of the unproductive are overtaking the producers. When that day ultimately comes we are all Doctor Zhivagos, sharing our property through government edicts. It's quite possible America will go broke first and the social welfare edifice be dismantled. On the other hand we could all be collectivized. Whatever the outcome, one thing stands as an historical certainty. We will either do away with socialism or socialism will do away with us.

CHAPTER THIRTY-TWO
SPRINTING DOWN THE ROAD TO RUIN

"We have enshrined a giant immorality as truth – that individual earnings belong to the collective rather than to those who produce them, and that we can in the name of the collective confiscate ever-larger portions of those earnings to advance our own individual lives and businesses in the form of pork, privileges, subsidies, loans, and entitlements." – Nelson Hultberg

"The essence and the glory of the free market is that individual firms and businesses, competing on the market, provide an ever-changing orchestration of efficient and progressive goods and services: continually improving products and markets, advancing technology, cutting costs, and meeting changing consumer demands as swiftly and as efficiently as possible." – Murray Rothbard

Mention the gold standard in Washington or New York and you're written off as the David Duke of finance. However, when Roosevelt abolished gold money, he opened Pandora's box. Under the gold standard the money supply grew at the rate that gold was mined (about 3% a year). Under the paper standard all such discipline was removed and discarded. This enabled politicians to introduce a vast array of social schemes that could now be paid for by inflating. It greased the skids for big government and the U.S. brand of socialism known as the mixed economy.

The fate of a nation's currency mirrors that country's financial health, prestige and influence. The big picture unfolding over the past hundred years and projecting a century into the future leaves little room for optimism. What grew the country was high savings, low taxes, capital accumulation, limited government and entrepreneurial freedom (*laissez faire*). Going forward we have low savings, high taxes, capital consumption, cancerous big government and regulatory zeal (interventionism). Instead of expanding what works, we embraced what never works.

As we careen from one economic crisis to another, our society will begin to unravel. The heavy footprint of government will grow more burdensome. Now laws and regulations will curb our freedoms. Rude civil servants will be even more obnoxious and unresponsive. Tax collectors will more aggressively seek out our wealth and new taxes will be spawned by a government desperate for funds to pay a growing army of the subsidized. Hatred of the affluent will be stoked by populist politicians. Within a few decades, the rich will be harassed and despised.

Today's leftists, radicals and liberals will never see that the social programs they created are the cause of inflation and economic retrogression. Although their vaunted socialistic schemes can never be paid for, they will still demand more. With the help of the media they will elect officials who resort to draconian measures of expropriation. In Argentina the government recently took over the banks and nationalized private retirement plans. A desperate government will do more harm than ever. The U.S. has embraced the monetary policies of a banana republic. Radical socialism is sure to follow.

As the economy collapses civil unrest will become unbearable. Demonstrations, riots, crime, strikes and social hatred will skyrocket as living standards plummet. The productive and the affluent will retreat into enclaves that promise security. Entrepreneurs will move offshore and immigrants return to their origins. Big government, the source of the nation's agony, will fail in its only important mission, to keep the citizenry safe. Eventually, Washington will become a cesspool of corruption, and New York a decrepit hulk of broken infrastructure populated by subsidized creatures howling for sustenance from the state.

The culture will coarsen further. As the subsidized underclass broadens, their morality and values will infect the media and corrupt our entertainment. Social injustice, poverty and inequality of incomes will dominate the news. Talking heads on TV will overwhelmingly stump for bigger government, higher taxes and more subsidies. Spokespersons for liberal social sympathy and compassionate conservatism will spew out nauseating prescriptions for helping a huge and growing class of ethically-challenged moochers. Rugged individualism and self- sufficiency will be replaced with weak-kneed shirkers who resonate helplessness.

The America we once knew will vanish under the onslaught of economic backwardness, social welfare, stifling bureaucracy, wealth transfer and chaotic behavior. If you think I'm exaggerating, guess again. The current rush into government bailouts and statist economic schemes sounds the alarm bell for this once great civilization. All such government programs and subsidies are socialistic. We have been adopting socialism for 75 years. There is no compromise between free market capitalism and socialism. Instead of trusting the market system, we have piecemeal adopted a left wing agenda. Unfortunately, there's no middle road. You have capitalism or you have the government fiasco we have today.

Socialism is killing our prosperity. Government rules and regulations have choked off Silicon Valley as the world's foremost hatchery of innovation. All the governments in the world, working in unison, could not create an Apple, a Google, an E-bay, a Cisco or a Hewlett-Packard. It's the entrepreneurs and free markets that make wealth and progress, not the politicians ladling out pork at the government trough.

Socialism doesn't work, can't work and never will work. Inevitably, it must lead into a new dark ages. That's where we're going in America - towards misery, mediocrity and perhaps extinction. Either we roll back socialism or we perish. So it was written by the great economists, so it shall be.

CHAPTER THIRTY-THREE
CHARACTER CRISIS

"If you are idle you are on the road to ruin, and there are few stopping places upon it. It is rather a precipice than a road." — Henry Ward Beecher

"Most of the major ills of the world have been caused by well-meaning people who ignored the principle of individual freedom, except as applied to themselves, and who were obsessed with fanatical zeal to improve the lot of mankind-in-the-mass through some pet formula of their own." — Henry Weaver

Writing about the decay of the American character (and culture), Charles J. Sykes tells us, "Something extraordinary is happening in American society. Crisscrossed by invisible trip wires of emotional, racial, sexual and psychological grievance, American life is increasingly characterized by the plaintive insistence, I am a victim... the mantra of the victims is the same: I am not responsible, it's not my fault."

The left has promoted massive subsidies and runaway social programs that encourage this mindset. People believe they deserve something for nothing. They believe they are victims. They rationalize a free ride. They are told the playing field isn't level, that merit is a scam, that values are subjective, that doing nothing is no better or worse than building and creating.

An employer sees it all: the fraudulent unemployment claims, the refusal to work, the unwillingness to do extra; the bogus lawsuits. Spurred by large legal awards, more and more people look for ways to sue, and depict themselves as victims.

Left-wing social policies sicken our behavior and corrupt our culture. People bend principles and sacrifice integrity to get as much as they can from the government. Giveaway programs encourage every imaginable sort of cheating and dishonesty. Wheeling and dealing in food stamps is a way of life. Lying and fraud are commonplace. Whenever you're dependent on the money, the end justifies the means.

Many people enrolled in one government program or another work part time for cash at either a legitimate job or illegal activity. By taking payments in cash, they don't show any income and can maintain their benefits. The numbers of people working the system this way are legion.

Money dispersed without any requirement to earn it seems to set off a defensive reaction wherein the recipients claim a right to the money, almost like a state pensioner or a person who has purchased an annuity. It creates an attitude problem. A friend tells of sitting in a doctor's office when an unemployed man became insulted because he was asked if he worked. He angrily emphasized that he would never work.

A certain segment of the population will always succumb to the lure of a free ride. When a bad back became a way to secure long-term workmen's compensation benefits, the number of bad backs per capita went through the roof. Payments to those who can't find work will snare many who can find work. Subsidies carry incentives that encourage more of the rewarded behavior. Payments for unemployment spread unemployment. Payments to alleviate poverty spread poverty.

Napoleon Hill said it best, "When a majority of the people of any nation give up their inherited prerogative right to make their own way through struggle, history shows clearly that the entire nation is in a tailspin of decay that inevitably must end in extinction."

CHAPTER THIRTY-FOUR
WITHOUT MERIT

"You know that great prejudice exists against all successful business enterprises – the more successful, the greater the prejudice."   – John D. Rockefeller

"Friedrich Hayek made the point that one of the keystones of socialism is the denial of individual responsibility. Thus, the crusade for socialism always included attacks on individual responsibility. For if individuals do not have free will, and are not responsible for their actions, then their lives must be controlled somehow – preferably by the state – according to the socialists. They must be regulated, regimented and controlled – for their own good."
                                                – Thomas J. DiLorenzo

"The vision of the left, full of envy and resentment, takes its worst toll on those at the bottom – whether black or white – who find in that paranoid vision an excuse for counterproductive and ultimately self-destructive attitudes and behavior."
                                                – Thomas Sowell

"Once a person becomes a government dependent, his moral standing to resist the expansion of government power is fatally compromised."   – James Bovard

Almost thirty years ago I left a comfortable family business and went to Miami to start a drinking water company. This endeavor was a huge personal struggle, full of financial peril, rejection, and anxiety. I devoted a chapter to this ordeal in my book, "The Start Up Entrepreneur." Fortunately, after more than a year of work and strain, a wealthy family made me an offer I couldn't refuse and I sold out to them. For a few months after that I was in the chips.

I returned to Minnesota and with a partner started Investment Rarities. In two years (1975) our money was gone and we were on the ropes. One crisis led to another. At a critical moment my partner buckled. He proclaimed our venture was defunct and tried to leave with one of our few potential assets. We had a falling out. I bought his stock for a small amount. He left me with a load of debt and unpaid bills.

At the moment we stared failure in the face he quit while I persisted. He had no faith in our future while I was sure we would ultimately succeed. Why? I had an enormous advantage over him. I had previously suffered through the despair and pain of near failure in my water business. This had strengthened me. My partner lacked persistence because he had no prior experience with struggle. In his previous enterprise he had made a lot of money without paying much of a price. Things had been easier for him.

The founder of U.S. Steel, Andrew Carnegie, strived for success in business so that he "should never again be called upon to endure such nights and days of wracking anxiety." I have suffered through these severe business droughts and cyclical downturns over the past three decades and one thing stands out. The struggles of life teach the truly valuable lessons. We learn little from good times, and virtually nothing from success. Emerson said it best. "When man [or woman]... is pushed, tormented, defeated, he has a chance to learn something; he has been put on his wits, on his manhood, he has gained facts, learns his ignorance, is cured of the insanity of conceit; has got moderation and real skill."

Now suppose that at the inception of my Miami water business there was a government program for young men that awarded me a large contract. My life would have been so much easier. I would have been an immediate success. At first glance this would have helped me enormously, but in reality it would have crippled me. I would have missed the lessons and struggles that had made me resourceful. Every bout of pain in life makes the next round more likely to be endured.

The government has programs and requirements that give money, or business contracts to women and minorities. These preferences supposedly help the recipient. But they do not. They simply relieve these people from learning the necessary lessons required to climb to the top and succeed on merit.

Those who oppose these government preferences are thought to be mean-spirited or reactionary. The media brands them as chauvinists or racists. In reality, most business owners or managers want a level playing field and would like to see minorities and women reach the upper levels of achievement. Most men in business want all people to experience success and are not in the least threatened by this prospect. But those of us who have struggled time and again know that this can never be accomplished with shortcuts. The government's subsidy programs will ruin the chances of minorities and women to take their place on the pinnacles of success. If you accept business contracts or money you didn't earn to speed your success, you undermine your long-term prospects and incur the dead opposite of what the government strives to accomplish. As Emerson instructs us, "Everything has its price - and if that price is not paid, not that thing but something else is obtained... it is impossible to get anything without its price."

Author Napoleon Hill advises, "The necessity for struggle is one of the clever devices through which nature forces individuals to expand, develop, progress, and become strong through resistance... We are forced to recognize that this great universal necessity for struggle must have a definite and useful purpose. That purpose is to force the individual to sharpen his wits, arouse his enthusiasm, build up his spirit of faith, gain definiteness of purpose, develop his power of will, inspire his faculty of imagination to give him new uses for old ideas and concepts... "

This philosophy is not just about getting ahead in business, it's also about getting ahead in life. Look at the long-term recipients of entitlements, subsidies and free housing. This unearned money was supposed to lift these people from poverty to a better, more prosperous life. In reality, it locked them into poverty.

If you get a job or promotion because of your race or gender, it is no different than a subsidy. You get something that you didn't earn, something for nothing. You are weaker for it than if you climbed the ladder by yourself. It may seem like a helping hand, but if it deprives you of skill and inner strength, it is a push backwards. Nothing good ever comes from getting something you didn't earn.

Now the government and the media encourages those who get entitlements to see themselves as victims. This is just one more horribly negative outcome of subsidies. Once trapped in the belief that you are a victim, you surrender your birthright to compete for the prizes of life. In the mind of the victims and their sponsors, everything controversial that happens in the country becomes just another insult and a plot to keep them from succeeding. Such perceptions inevitably become reality.

It's not just the underclass that suffers from something for nothing. A corollary exists with the children of wealthy people who shield their offspring from economic struggle. If you are affluent and want to harm your children, give them all the money they will ever need. If you leave them your fortune before they've made their own way, they will be weaker for it. Rich or poor, insulate them from life's struggles and you will fashion people who cannot stand on their own, cannot build, accomplish or create. Herein lies the principal threat to American freedom, prosperity and greatness.

CHAPTER THIRTY-FIVE
PARENTS OF THE YEAR

"Even those government programs that do the most damage today were devised with the best of intentions. Good intentions however, seldom survive the realities of the programs in practice." — Michael D. Tanner

"Instead of solving economic problems, government welfare socialism created monstrous moral and spiritual problems – the kind of problems that are inevitable when individuals turn responsibility for their lives over to others." — Star Parker

"Somehow, the fact that more poor people are on welfare, receiving more generous payments, does not seem to have made this country a nice place to live – not even for the poor on welfare, whose condition seems not noticeably better than when they were poor and off welfare. Something appears to have gone wrong; a liberal and compassionate social policy has bred all sorts of unanticipated and perverse consequences." — Irving Kristol

We condensed a recent news article in the Minneapolis newspaper.

"Multiple children were drinking alcohol and some were reportedly smoking marijuana in the house where a 3-year-old girl was found Monday night with a 0.12 percent blood-alcohol level.

"The children's mothers are sisters, age 32 and 31, each have six children ranging from 1 to 15. The petitions in juvenile court describe a chaotic scene where police found the toddler unresponsive, 'fresh vomit all over the house' and drunken adults yelling to each other.

"The 3-year-old drank Windsor Canadian whisky after the girl's 14-year-old brother gave it to her in a cup and said it was juice," court documents said.

"A 5-year-old daughter told authorities that she and three cousins, two of whom are 4 and 6, also drank alcohol.

"According to court documents: Police officers noticed a 'thick haze of smoke' and a strong smell of marijuana in the home. Children were smoking marijuana. Officers also found liquor spilled on the floor and soiled clothes and food strewn about the house.

"The 3-year-old's eyes were wide open but were glazed over and she was unresponsive.

"Officers found a juvenile male who appeared intoxicated and smelled strongly of alcohol crawling out a window. Adults home at the time – police have said there were four – were drunk and unable to dress the children.

"One mother was previously convicted of second-degree murder in 1997 and sentenced to five years in prison in the stabbing death of a woman. She has been the subject of five child-protection reports dating to 2000, including a finding of sexual abuse and endangerment regarding one of her daughters.

"The other mother's record includes theft convictions. She had multiple contacts with County Child Protection, most stemming from domestic assaults."

If you think pre-schoolers smoking marijuana are a rarity, you're wrong. It's not uncommon among the urban underclass. That says nothing about sexual promiscuity, thievery, drug peddling and violence among pre-teens and young adults. It's a social mess of staggering proportions brought to you by our liberal social thinkers and bureaucrats. Social agencies are so incompetent and corrupt they will not remove an innocent child or even a tiny infant from abusive, chemically dependent mothers with scumbag boyfriends. Sexual and physical abuse goes unnoticed and ignored. These brutes are killing infants and children accidentally or on purpose with alarming frequency. Unfortunately, little kids who survive these toxic mothers, relatives and boyfriends are likely to grow up to be hoodlums themselves. This is the circle of dependency and crime that government is purchasing for you with your own money. Your tax dollars fund social programs that produce grossly dysfunctional criminals and addicts. Unfortunately, your grandchildren face the prospect of life among swelling numbers of remorseless criminals.

Our cities are full of similar horror stories. Social programs that pay unwed mothers for every child they have only encourages the least responsible to have multiple births. By some estimates, the birth rate of the underclass is three times greater than that of the general population. There are a million little kids in our country whose character is being ruined by lack of love, chaotic behavior and bad example. Alcoholics, drug addicts, prostitutes and criminals are not fit to raise children. Social workers should be tarred and feathered for leaving babies with these lowlifes. If you took these infants away from the clowns raising them and put them in good homes, twenty years from now they'd be graduating from college instead of going to prison.

We're worrying about the wrong things in this country. What could be more important than protecting little children from criminally negligent adults? What could be more important than transferring kids from behavioral hellholes into loving, secure homes or even orphanages? Prohibitions against interracial adoptions are the insane handiwork of liberal social workers. The American people will step up and save these children if given a chance. For that to happen, the progressives must see the gravity of the problem and admit their policies have caused this social mayhem. Frankly, I think they would rather turn their back on these kids than admit their socialist claptrap is bankrupt.

CHAPTER THIRTY-SIX
LIBERAL LEGACY

"Transfer payments discourage the recipients from earning income in the present and from investing in their potential to earn income in the future. People respond to a reduced cost of idleness by choosing to be idle more often."

– Robert Higgs

"Government does not have magic powers. In fact, the opposite is true; it is the least effective agency invented by man."

– Robert Prechter

I turned my mud-covered Suburban onto the gravel road leading through the Indian reservation. In the back two mallards lay on a bag of decoys. They had flown into the Saskatchewan pothole I had hunted earlier that day. I planned to give them to Bird Lady. Each year I dropped off a few plump mallards for Bird Lady and her daughters.

It was close to one in the afternoon when I turned up Bird Lady's driveway. Her house sat on the top of a knoll a quarter mile off the main gravel. I passed the run-down bungalows of her daughters and pulled into the barren, weedy yard. A dozen oversized chickens scurried away.

I walked up the porch steps and knocked on the door. No one came. I thought about Bird Lady as I waited. She had been a beautiful woman once, but the ravages of age and alcohol had withered her. I pounded louder. It quickly dawned on me that I had come too early. Bird Lady slept and she would not get up now.

I glanced at the daughters' modern bungalows that had deteriorated into hovels. Rags were stuffed into holes in windows and siding. Curtains, towels and sheets covered the windows. A beat-up car sat in front of one. Neither would the daughters rise. In past years I had noted that the daughters showed signs of advanced alcoholism. Their appearance had deteriorated. They could never seem to look me in the eye and although I had tried to engage one of them in conversation her hang-dog expression revealed a deep-seated sense of inferiority. Their children were in school today. On weekends the children would be outside in the morning at unsupervised play while the elders slept.

In all of North America nothing is more pathetic or sad than the Indian reservations. They are laboratories for a social experiment that has harmed the character of people who were once the most self-sufficient on earth. Never in history has an entire category of people sunk to such levels of helplessness, addiction and degradation.

Responsibility for this wretched predicament does not lie with the 7th Cavalry or the gory spectacle at Wounded Knee. It lies with modern social scientists, bureaucrats, and leftists who insist on giving these people a monthly stipend that leaves them unchallenged, unmotivated and bored senseless. People grow primarily through economic struggle. Subsidies discourage this growth. They retard human potentiality.

I rolled the Suburban down the drive, away from Bird Lady and her daughters. I passed dozens of other bungalows, some occupied, some abandoned or destroyed. No cars passed me. Some people would not be up for several hours. I turned it over in my mind. They must go to bed close to dawn. What weird behavioral syndrome does welfare unleash that keeps these people and others on the permanent dole up until 4 or 5 in the morning, and asleep all day? How can they raise children on such a schedule?

That's the dirty little secret in all of this welfare nonsense. The children raise themselves. The outcome of this gross neglect, where eight-year-olds raise three-year-olds, can be seen in the chronic rates of crime, abuse, addiction and social disintegration endemic to the subsidized. The little children, the innocents, the tiny ones who crave love and nurturing, get no more attention than the dog. They play outside through the day, a bag of chips for breakfast, a Pepsi and a Ho-Ho for their lunch, unsupervised and unloved.

Twenty years ago I stood in the parking lot of a restaurant in The Pas, a small community in Northern Manitoba. I was fishing with a friend and I waited outside while he used the washroom. A large bus had pulled into the lot and disgorged its passengers. The front door of the bus was open, the driver reading a newspaper. Suddenly around the corner came a small Indian boy of about four. He was dressed neatly in shorts and he was a child of such remarkable beauty that my eyes became glued to him. He walked to the bus and stood in the sunlight, looking up into the doorway, fascinated by what he saw, radiating innocence and charm. Around the corner came his father. I glanced his way but riveted my attention back on the boy. The father encouraged him to take a few steps onto the bus. It was clear the boy had never entered a bus before and this was a high adventure for him. He took a step up and then another and surveyed the interior of the bus. As he stepped back down I stood fascinated by his angelic demeanor that had prompted this reverential episode.

His father called to him and I looked back at the man. It startled me. The father was my age. Like the boy, he too had been handsome, but too much whiskey had left heavy lines and creases in his face. His red and sunken eyes stared out from his damaged features and his curled posture spoke of intoxication. I looked back at the boy and in a moment of dread I saw what this little angel would become. I stood silently and fought the tears.

Our perceptions about welfare and subsidies are shifting at warp speed. The American people have come to understand the devastating effects of welfare even as the left has hardened their views. Advocates of the current welfare disaster remain inflexible in the face of the evidence.

Once upon a time there was a simple, honest, disciplined, happy, self-sufficient tribal culture. It exists no more. The white man ruined that. However, it was not the loss of their land or the subtle imprisonment on reservations that did in the Indians and their culture. It was the monthly checks. The dole kills the spirit and destroys character. Subsidies are behavioral poison.

Bird Lady would have been a different person had she been required to make her own way in life. She had the potential. You could see the intelligence and humor in her eyes. She liked my visits. She could have been somebody. What a waste. Yes, there are exceptions to Bird Lady. A few Indians farm and work successfully. But the mind-numbing rate of alcoholism on the reservations approaches ninety percent. A pox on all who fail to see the cause.

CHAPTER THIRTY-SEVEN
DRINKING THE PROGRESSIVE POISON

"Peace and prosperity are inversely proportional to the level of taxation."
– John A. Pugsley

"The greatest destroyer of capital, the greatest anti-capitalist, and therefore the greatest detractor to mankind is the state."
– Jerome F. Smith

"Highly graduated taxation realizes most completely the supreme danger of democracy, creating a state of things in which one class imposes on another burdens which it is not asked to share, and impels the State into vast schemes of extravagance, under the belief that the whole costs will be thrown upon others."
– W.E.H. Lecky

The first thing liberals want to do when elected to office is raise taxes. They especially want to punish the rich. In fact, they prefer taxes to be so high they become a disguised means of confiscation. They overlook the fact that people with money provide the savings, capital and investments necessary to foster new business and grow existing enterprise. High taxes are a penalty on progress.

Hilary Clinton once told a group of wealthy people, "We're going to take things away from you on behalf of the common good." Of course, the liberals and socialists want to determine exactly what the public good is going to be. So far, their efforts on behalf of the public good have led to one failed socialist scheme after another. The philosopher Leonard Read wrote, "statism is but socialized dishonesty; it is feathering the nests of some with feathers coercively plucked from others on a grand scale. There is no moral difference between the act of a pickpocket and the progressive income tax or any other social program." The writer, Craig Cantoni put it this way. "Those on the receiving end of a public good like the public good more than those on the paying end."

Liberals believe an inexhaustible fund exists that can be tapped endlessly to pay for government social programs. Tax the rich and give it to a long line of moochers, pork barrel hustlers and ne'er-do-wells. These funds would otherwise have been employed as additional capital indispensable to economic progress. When taxes become too high, capital is consumed rather than accumulated, and profits, wage rates and living standards fall. The progressive tax system favored by the left eventually liquidates itself. It kills the goose that laid the golden egg.

The great economist Murray Rothbard put it this way: "... soaking the rich to subsidize the poor, does no such thing. In fact, soaking the rich would have disastrous effects, not just for the rich but for the poor and middle classes themselves. For it is the rich who provide a proportionately greater amount of saving, investment capital, entrepreneurial foresight, and financing of technological innovation that has brought the United States to by far the highest standard of living – for the mass of the people – of any country in history. Soaking the rich would not only be profoundly immoral, it would drastically penalize the very virtues: thrift, business foresight, and investment that have brought about our remarkable standard of living."

All of the huge, expensive social programs run by government are hatched by liberals. Public housing, Medicare, the varied subsidies of the "great society" all came from the left. This orgy of vote buying worked to the benefit of liberals who were rewarded by voters with public office. The other side took notice and began to climb on board. Now conservatives promote huge Federal subsidies. It's become a race to see who can come up with unique ways to dispense benefits. Republicans have drunk the liberal poison.

The founding fathers established a government to keep us safe inside the country and to protect us from enemies without. In a modern society we justify adding government protection of health, safety and the environment. Beyond that, it's all subsidies and spending. We take money from those who earn it and give it to those who don't. Would you voluntarily donate your money to a major corporation to subsidize gasohol or give it to abusive mothers whose delinquent children may someday be a threat to your safety?

Subsidies are ruining us because they are morally bankrupt. They corrupt what they touch. They cause the huge government deficits that must be financed through raw inflating. When you superimpose the cost of war and other emergencies on a runaway social budget, you can be certain the dollar will be debased. The liberals would pare down defense spending, and you may or may not disagree. However, their bias is to always increase social spending. That's why subsidies are running away, and they will do so until the government or the taxpayers go broke, whichever comes first.

CHAPTER THIRTY-EIGHT
MISSING THE BIG PICTURE

"No one has more than scratched the surface when it comes to understanding the miracle of the market."
– Leonard E. Read

"Whatever men live for, today most live only because of the market order."
– Friedrich Hayek

"Politicians never accuse you of 'greed' for wanting other people's money – only for wanting to keep your own money."
– Joseph Sobran

The exceedingly liberal Minneapolis newspaper ran a recent editorial on baseball. They referred to Yankee owner, George Steinbrener, as greedy. Liberals love to describe successful people as greedy. They prefer the type of business person personified by Wesley Mouch, a character in Ayn Rand's novel, *Atlas Shrugged*. Mr. Mouch was proud of the fact that his heavily subsidized company had never made a profit.

George Steinbrener does what is necessary to win. He doesn't break any laws and the fans reward him with a profit. Baseball salaries may be out of the park, but blame much of that on inflation, players unions and agents. You don't have to love the Yankees, but you have to admire their success. George fields a winner and fills the ballpark. Isn't that his job?

Virtually anyone who makes a lot of money gets written off by the left as greed driven. Most of the animosity stems from envy. The sight of people who have made money through greater ability bothers them. They credit this solely to luck, dishonesty or greed. They forget that under the market system you acquire wealth by serving others. Consumers are king and their buying decisions determine who gets rich and who loses out. Everyone has the same opportunity under capitalism and most of us start from the same place. Those with the ability to provide products and services to the greatest number of people make the most money.

Editorial writers for liberal newspapers don't fare as well at money making as high-tech innovators. However, they prefer to believe that this income disparity comes through exploitation or luck. They want to believe that someone goes without because someone else gets rich. They root for higher taxes to level incomes. But the money earned by wealthy entrepreneurs does not cause anyone's poverty. The same process that makes entrepreneurs rich also satisfies the people's wants and needs in the best and cheapest way. Business standardizes our consumption and enjoyment and every citizen shares in these material blessings.

Envy and ignorance of how free market capitalism works account for both the Leninists of yesterday and the liberals of today. Their animosity towards profit-making has saddled business with a host of regulations and social requirements that competitors in other parts of the world don't have to deal with. Liberals love government and its multiple cures for every social ailment. They fail to realize that public social programs exhaust the resources of the nation and corrupt the citizenry.

Sad to say, I have friends, and even relatives, who vote for political candidates on the left. Generally, they have embraced liberalism because of one or more social issues that concern them. Unfortunately, they allow this narrow perspective to override the great historical struggle of our time between socialism and capitalism (government control vs. free market). They erroneously believe this conflict to be irrelevant or no longer germane. For this belief, they risk exchanging their prosperity and freedom for poverty and statism.

Many believe we have reached a compromise between socialism and capitalism. Not so. There is no middle ground. There is only transition from one to the other. In America, that transition leads down the road to big government and lower living standards.

Hostility towards business runs deep on the left. On college campuses professors pontificate about robber barons and corporate crooks. Their heroes are never business pioneers or innovative entrepreneurs. They would rather enshrine a Che Guevara than a Ray Kroc or Steve Jobs. Che, that hero of leftist lore once claimed, "The oppressor must be killed mercilessly....the revolutionary must become an efficient and selective killing machine." Contrast that with a capitalist hero of today, George Gilder, who said, "'Do unto others as you would have them do unto you,' and 'Give and you will be given unto,' are the central rules of the life of enterprise."

Support for the left means far more than promoting your personal social cause. It's a vote for big government, overregulation, statism and less freedom. It's a vote for the government to take more and more of what people earn. As much as anything, it's a vote to put all commerce under the thumb of politicians and government to the point they die off like so many dinosaurs. Voting for a liberal may keep your social cause alive and well, but if the left gains enough influence, you are going to hate your low wages, empty shelves and old car.

CHAPTER THIRTY-NINE
LOONY LEFTISTS

"A great civilization is not conquered from without until it has destroyed itself from within. The essential causes of Rome's decline lay in her people, morals, her class struggle, her failing trade, her bureaucratic despotism, her stifling taxes, her consuming wars."
– Will Durant

"Inflation comes about because our politicians and bankers create billions of new paper dollars out of nowhere. It is, in essence, the same thing as counterfeiting, which if done by a private citizen would result in a jail sentence."
– Nelson Hultberg

"Chesterton spoke of 'the modern and morbid habit of always sacrificing the normal to the abnormal.' It would be hard to sum up liberalism more succinctly."
– Joseph Sobran

In the past few years a lot of books promoting atheism and attacking religion made it onto the best seller list. Most of these authors are liberals and their books are embraced and applauded by the left. It's the hot new thing.

If you're not worried about this trend, maybe you should be. Here's what author Dinesh D'Souza writes: "Psychologist Nicholas Humphrey argued in a recent lecture that just as Amnesty International works to liberate political prisoners around the world, secular teachers and professors should work to free children from the damaging influence of their parents' religious instruction. 'Parents, correspondingly, have no god-given license to enculturate their children in whatever ways they personally choose: no right to limit the horizons of their children's knowledge, to bring them up in an atmosphere of dogma and superstition, or to insist they follow the straight and narrow paths of their own faith.'

"Philosopher Richard Rorty argued that secular professors in the universities ought 'to arrange things so that students who enter as bigoted, homophobic religious fundamentalists will leave college with views more like our own.' Rorty noted that students are fortunate to find themselves 'under the benevolent Herrschaft [dominion] of people like me, and to have escaped the grip of their frightening, vicious, dangerous parents.' Indeed, parents who send their children to college should recognize that as professors 'we are going to go right on trying to discredit you in the eyes of your children, trying to strip your fundamentalist religious community of dignity, trying to make your views seem silly rather than discussible.'"

If it's not one thing it's another with liberals. In addition to this anti-religious bias, they've been cozying up to radical Islam, slandering the rich, knocking Israel, promoting an extreme environmental agenda, finding racism everywhere, despising capitalism, hating white males and lobbying for the biggest tax increase in history. The writer Joe Sobran put it best, "Liberalism's fatal flaw... is that it has no permanent norms, only a succession of enthusiasms espoused by minor prophets. Each of these seems like a hot new idea to liberals, but soon goes to irksome and destructive extremes."

CHAPTER FORTY
MORE MISES

"As crisis after crisis torments the American people, each gives ample opportunity to reiterate what we have been sharing all along: do not look to your oppressor, the government, for solutions to the very problems it created."
– Christine Smith

"Under capitalism men provide for themselves, while under Socialism they are provided for."
– Ludwig von Mises

"A fact rarely suspected, let alone understood, is that businessmen are by no means the chief beneficiaries of the free market, private ownership, limited government way of life. Many business ventures fail entirely. Who then are the beneficiaries? The masses!"
– Leonard E. Read

Never before have the middle class and the affluent been at greater financial risk. The Federal Reserve is moving ahead with a plan to target the rate of inflation and make inflating a permanent policy. Not that it doesn't inflate incessantly now. This plan only serves to show how deranged monetary policy has become. It would be better if they truthfully declared that they intend to establish a policy that destroys the savings of the people, debases the dollar and ruins the retirement years of the elderly.

The great Austrian school economist Ludwig von Mises was the foremost critic of inflation. In 1967 he wrote, "Inflationism is a government policy of increasing the quantity of money in order to enable the government to spend more than the funds provided by taxation and borrowing. Such 'deficit spending' is nowadays, as everybody knows the characteristic signature of the U.S. government's policies." He added, "There is no reason to be proud of deficit spending or to call it progress."

Mises' main complaint against this inflating was the damage it did to the people who saved. In 1960 he wrote, "One of the main achievements of the capitalistic system is the opportunity it offers to the masses of citizens to save and thereby improve their material well being... the value of all kinds of deposits, bonds and insurance policies is inseparably linked to the purchasing power of the dollar. A policy of creeping inflation... is a policy against the vital material interests of the common man. It hurts seriously those judicious and conscientious earners of wages and salaries who are intent upon improving their own and their families' lot by thrift... It is... diabolic... for more and more government spending to be financed by credit expansion. The bill for such government extravagance is always footed by the most industrious and provident people. It is their claims [savings] that are shrinking with the dollar's purchasing power."

Because Mises was Austrian his earliest arguments were not translated or understood in the U.S. Nevertheless his accomplishments were prodigious. Among them was his argument that Communism must fail because free market prices were unavailable to direct their production. They were in the dark on how much of anything to produce. When they ultimately collapsed it was widely acknowledged that he had been right.

During Mises' lifetime he saw the arguments of John Maynard Keynes become influential. In 1951 Mises wrote, "The triumphs of Lord Keynes' last book, *The General Theory*, was instantaneous…it has become the gospel of the self-styled progressives all over the world. Today many universities simply teach Keynesianism. It is really paradoxical. Nobody can any longer fail to realize what is needed most is more saving and capital accumulation and that the inflationary and expansionist polices are on the verge of complete breakdown. But the students are still taught the dangers of saving and the blessing of inflating."

Mises emphasized the inevitability of a crisis if the inflationary policies practiced by the government and the Federal Reserve were continued. However, not only have they continued they have expanded to a point that would no doubt shock the great economist. In 1951 he wrote, "Continued inflation inevitably leads to catastrophe." He indicted Washington, "It is government interference that has destroyed money in the past and it is government interference that is destroying money again."

Mises also scorned politicians, Treasury and Federal Reserve officials who claimed to be intent on thwarting inflation. "Those who pretend to fight inflation are in fact only fighting the inevitable consequences of inflation, rising prices…They try to keep prices low while firmly committed to a policy of increasing the quantity of money that must necessarily make them soar."

Mises culminated his arguments against inflating with dire warnings on where the monetary policies of today will lead. Bear in mind that Mises through his many books and trenchant arguments is recognized as a towering genius in his field. His warnings should be heeded by anyone interested in their future security.

"It must be remembered that inflation is not a policy that can last. If inflation and credit expansion are not stopped in time, they result in a more and more accelerated drop in the monetary unit's purchasing power, and in skyrocketing commodity prices until the inflated money becomes entirely worthless and the whole government-manipulated currency system collapses. In our age, this has happened to the monetary regime of various countries."

He further warned, "Inflationism is not a variety of economic policies. It is an instrument of destruction; if not stopped very soon, it destroys the market entirely." Finally, here are Mises' comments that apply to the Krugmanites, the progressive politicians and the Washington monetary gang: "Inflationism cannot last; if not radically stopped in time, it must lead inexorably to a complete breakdown. It is an expedient of people who do not care a whit for the future of their nation and its civilization. It is the policy of Madame de Pompadour, the mistress of the French King Louis XV – *Apres nous le deluge* (after us the deluge)."

We are so far down the road of money creation that the final outcome appears inevitable. Our leaders are clueless when it comes to Professor Mises and his warnings. When a problem arises they inflate all the more. At least a few of us have the opportunity to take him seriously. Many new people are beginning to recognize these dangers. The problem, however, is that as more people abandon the dollar, prices will rise further, thus accelerating the rate of inflation. Any big jump in prices this year will feed the fears of runaway inflation and move it closer.

CHAPTER FORTY-ONE
TEN REASONS NOT TO RAISE TAXES

"Once we realize that government doesn't work, we'll know that the only way to improve government is by reducing its size – by doing away with laws, by getting rid of programs, by making government spend and tax less, by reducing government as far as we can." – Harry Browne

"Congress can raise taxes because it can persuade a sizable fraction of the populace that somebody else will pay." – Milton Friedman

"The institution of taxation is not a civilized but a barbaric method to fund anything... it amounts to... a gross violation of human liberty." – Tibor Machan

Private business and entrepreneurs make much better use of their profits than government. Bureaucrats can't introduce new products and services, create jobs or wealth. Every dollar taxed off by government hurts economic growth. High taxes are a penalty on progress.

Low taxes spur growth. The fastest growing economy in Europe is Albania with a 10% tax rate. Texas, with no state income tax, is creating 45% of the new jobs in America. There is no known example of higher taxes improving an economy. However, lowering taxes invariably increases prosperity.

Taxes are already high. It's a fabrication to claim that high income earners do not pay their fair share. There is no escaping the requirement to pay 42% of ordinary income to the government. By historical standards this is punitive. It's close to the highest in the world.

High taxes erode charity. The generosity of the American people is legendary. Now charitable acts are taken over and directed by the government. Our charitable givers increasingly let the government fund the giving. Furthermore, high taxes mean less money for donations.

There is a moral issue. Why does someone who is down on his luck have a right to the earnings of others? What moral right does a corn grower have to my money? Isn't it wrong for one person to benefit at the expense of another? Helping people should be a voluntary act free of government coercion.

Business has its ups and downs. High taxes make it difficult for a company to build cash reserves. Without a cushion in downturns more companies go out of business. The government has eroded their staying power and thereby increased unemployment.

The government cannot measure the results of their taxing and spending. Private corporations measure success through profit or loss. Government has no such objective standard. The tendency in government is to equate success with spending more while private companies cut costs.

For profitable companies and big earners reducing taxes became an obsession. Too much time is wasted on this exercise, deductions are stretched, and unworkable tax shelters are sometimes employed.

High taxes act as a barrier to companies opening branches, distribution centers or offices in a state. Low tax states are winning the competition for businesses that are expanding.

It takes hard work and struggle to make a profit. Nevertheless, the tax system punishes successful, productive people and rewards those who are unproductive. No nation can prosper for long with such perverse incentives. Yes, a certain level of taxes are necessary but the current high tax regime is misguided, unfair and counterproductive.

CHAPTER FORTY-TWO
EXPROPRIATE THE CAPITALISTS

"The ability of the market to serve society has been and is continually being undermined by the attacks leveled by its ideological opponents."
– Israel M. Kirzner

"The more 'adequate' we make relief, the more people we are going to find willing to get on it and stay on it indefinitely. The more we try to make sure that everybody really in need of relief gets it, the more certain we can be that we are also giving it to people who neither need nor deserve it."
– Henry Hazlitt

"Experience shows that nothing is operated with less economy and with more waste of labor and material of every kind than public services and undertakings. Private enterprise on the other hand naturally induces the owner to work with the greatest economy in his own interest."
– Ludwig von Mises

Columnist Vasko Kohlmayer quotes Michael Moore in his film, *Capitalism: A Love Story*. "Capitalism is an evil, and you cannot regulate evil... you have to eliminate it and replace it with something that is good for all people."

Kohlmayer goes on to say, "Capitalism is increasingly cast as the great villain of our time. It's blamed for exploitation, poverty, fraud, alienation, crime, racism and nearly everything else."

Kohlmayer continues, "The bad rap could not be more undeserved. Rather than mankind's scourge, capitalism has been its greatest benefactor. It is, in fact, the only socio-economic system that can provide ordinary people with dignified and prosperous lives. It was only with the advent of capitalism that the common man was able to escape the penury and filth of his existence to which he had been previously consigned. Until then, the lives of most people were short, hard and miserable. Today, as if by miracle, we can enjoy greater comforts and ease of life than the kings of the past."

As author Lew Rockwell confirms, "Capitalism, and capitalism alone, has rescued the human race from degrading poverty, rampant sickness and early death."

Kohlmayer points out, "Capitalism is responsible for nearly everything that makes human existence easy and comfortable. The automobile, the supermarket, the personal computer, the washing machine, the hammer-drill, the iPhone, the airplane, the TV set, chewing gum, electricity and countless other good things have all been birthed and mass produced by capitalism."

Rockwell agrees, "The profit system balances human needs with the availability of all the world's resources, unleashes the amazing power of human creativity, and works to meet the material needs of every member of society at the least possible cost. It does this through exchange, cooperation, competition, entrepreneurship, and all the institutions that make possible capitalism – the most productive economic system this side of heaven."

Says Kohlmayer, "Because of its immense wealth generating power, people who live in capitalist societies enjoy rising standards of living and material affluence. Conversely, those who live in non-capitalist societies invariably experience the opposite... The rule always holds: Capitalist societies are invariably prosperous. Non-capitalist ones are always poor."

What's going on with Michael Moore and the Hollywood left? Actors like Sean Penn and Danny Glover are kissing up to the socialist dictator Chavez in Venezuela. They seem to prefer a government strong man who will confiscate the property and wealth of those who earned it and transfer it to illiterates in exchange for their votes. This must also be their vision for America. These are dangerous trends. If they were to prevail, those of us who aim to prosper will be on the outside looking in. Capitalists may even become like the Russian kulaks (farmers) who were exterminated by Lenin and Stalin in order to implement collective farming. Socialists and communists have often murdered those who disagreed with them. As I mentioned earlier Che Guevara said, "The oppressors must be killed mercilessly... the revolutionary must become an efficient and selective killing machine."

Michael Moore has a lot more in common with the Bolsheviks than anyone would like to think. The author David Horowitz (a former associate of the Black Panthers who experienced the Panther's murder of a friend) has become the leading authority on the radical left.

He puts it this way. "It's interesting that we have words like 'neo-Nazi' to describe post-Hitler Nazis, and 'neo-conservative' to describe liberals who left the Democratic Party when it took a sharp turn to the left, but not 'neo-Communist' to describe the massive numbers of people on the left – and among them very influential people – who share, almost to the jot and title, the old communist view of capitalism, and are prepared to act on that perception... Neo-communists like Moore share the old communists' antipathy for the United States and sympathy for its enemies, even enemies as evil as Iran and Hezbollah.

"A neo-communist is someone who is convinced that race, class, and gender hierarchies make it not only legitimate but necessary to describe America as a "white supremacist" society. Neo-communists believe that a revolution is necessary (if not opportune at the moment), that the Constitution is a disposable document, and that America's communist and Islamo-fascist enemies (Iran, Venezuela, Cuba, Nicaragua, Hezbollah, the PLO and Hamas) are freedom fighters or at least on the right side of the armageddon that faces us.

"These are views shared by *The Nation* magazine, by Commonsense.org, by the Indymedia crowd, by the social justice movement, by the majority of the Black Caucus and the Progressive Caucus on the Democratic side in Congress and by tens of thousands of university professors who indoctrinate their students in these pernicious ideologies every day. They are the views held by the leaders of ACORN, the SEIU, AFCSME, and other leftwing unions, by radical feminists, by organizations like MALDEF and La Raza, by the ACLU and the Center for Constitutional Rights... This coalition, which I have called the 'unholy alliance,' presents a massive threat to America's security and its individual freedoms and its free market system."

Commenting on Michael Moore's new film, which he calls lying propaganda, columnist Walter Williams sums it up: "Not withstanding all of the demagoguery, it is capitalism not socialism that made us a great country and it's socialism that will be our undoing."

CHAPTER FORTY-THREE
TOO LATE

"The stark truth is that as long as the welfare state makes it possible for young women – or teenage girls – to have children without a husband and survive without a job, out-of-wedlock births will remain ruinously high, and the inner city will continue to be marked by crime, poverty, and despair." – David Boaz

"The welfare state has bred a generation of obnoxious, drug-addled criminals and ne'er-do-wells. It has also, incidentally, burdened what was once the world's biggest, most dynamic economy with the dead weight of an obstructive and vastly expensive state machine." – Martin Durkin

It's easy to talk about trimming social programs and reducing the deficit but it's not going to happen. Once these programs are in place too many people come to depend on them. Taking away food stamps, public housing or disability payments would inspire the media to write an orgy of sob stories. Heartless politicians on the right would feel too much heat. Look at the furor in Wisconsin over a few simple reforms for overpaid government employees. An angry TV commercial from AARP almost promises to lynch anyone who contemplates Medicare reform.

The subsidies aren't going to end until the money has lost most of its value and national bankruptcy makes borrowing and printing impossible. Even onerous levels of taxation won't help. First will come runaway inflation and then an intractable depression and perhaps a new dark ages if the progressives stay in power.

The hardest programs to cut are those that are the costliest. The art of keeping people alive has broken new ground and it is terribly expensive. The liberal party wants the guy who lives under a bridge to get the same heart transplant or autoimmune drug treatment as a working man who pays for his health insurance. The new drug and medical technologies have expanded mightily because of subsidies and their immediate embrace by government health care programs. It's a Catch-22 and it's one of the main reasons we're going broke.

You can't begin to imagine how much money is frittered away on useless government initiatives. In Minneapolis, last month an organization called Northside Achievement Zone won a $28 million dollar federal grant to improve an impoverished neighborhood. A group of liberals were pictured in the newspaper applauding and our two left wing Senators were on hand. Certainly the supporters mean well but the fact that throwing money at the problem doesn't work never seems to register.

The CEO was in tears as she pointed out the many needs of the neighborhood. This is an area of high crime, drugs, alcoholism, broken families, prostitution and delinquency. Most of these people are subsidized and on welfare. Trillions have been spent trying to cure neighborhoods like this and if anything, they have grown worse. It's highly likely that federal subsidies are more the cause of these behavioral problems than the cure. If you don't have to work, boredom begets pathologies.

As for the $28 million I put it in perspective this way. Since 1973 when I started my company we have had up to 300 employees (in 1980). All of us have worked hard to improve our circumstances. We have all paid taxes in a timely fashion. In all those 38 years of hard work all of us have probably paid the government close to $28 million. It takes a lot of effort to get that amount of taxes. Nevertheless, the government dispenses it with little realization of the work and struggle involved.

It wouldn't be so bad if they were just spending our tax money. They can't get along on that. They have to borrow the $28 million and if they've borrowed too much they will have to print the $28 million. Multiply that ten thousand times over and you will see why we are dead in the water. Nothing is going to repeal our social spending but the inability to get the money. Some day the government checks will not go out. Imagine the dimensions of that collapse. Sadly, it's too late for anything else.

CHAPTER FORTY-FOUR
REBIRTH OF THE RUGGED INDIVIDUALIST

"All the impoverishing effects of socialism are with us in the U.S.: reduced levels of investment and saving, the misallocation of resources, the overutilitzation and vandalization of factors of production, and the inferior quality of products and services."
— Hans-Hermann Hoppe

"If any behavior needs to be reined in, it should be the propensity of people to use the political system to take other people's money."
— Jeffrey A. Singer

After years of wasteful spending European countries have no choice but to accept austerity. It will either be forced upon them or it will be voluntary. These countries (including the U.S.) remind me of people who suddenly make a lot of money, get bigheaded and blow their fortune on high living. Usually they wind up suffering through financial reversals and a lengthening period of personal austerity. They are humbled by these struggles. Often we hear that these painful experiences changed them for the better.

Perhaps the same rules apply to countries. A country that experiences austerity and bankruptcy may emerge from this humiliating period with its people more self-sufficient and its industries more productive. In that sense this national comeuppance, with all its agonies may be a good thing. The people come to understand there is no free lunch. They work more and play less. Behavior and character improve.

Here in the U.S. we have reached a level of excess that betrays our legacy and ensures our collapse. Public and private debt, runaway government spending and fiat money have hit the wall. We can't go back and going forward invites retribution. A national humbling and painful austerity are inevitable. The ferocity of the crisis will be correlated to the degree of excess, so it will be large and painful.

Taxation will be high but it will harvest little. The handouts will have to go. No more green energy, farm and corporate subsidies. No more food stamps, housing, welfare, unemployment and disability. Reduced veterans' benefits, Social Security and Medicare are certain. Student loans are no more. Pension and retirement programs shrivel and consumers freeze up. Bankruptcies explode and famous financial firms fold when the government's lifeline runs dry.

Crony capitalism dies. Government layoffs turn into an avalanche. Underfunded lobbyists, foundations, think tanks, government consultants, trial lawyers and political demonstrators disappear. Charitable donations plunge and the recipients of charity are hard pressed. Property crime increases. Austerity lays the nation low.

Jobs become more valuable and the work ethic improves. Lower wages bring more jobs. The culture changes. Entertainment wanes and self-improvement gains. Art becomes understandable and music harkens to an earlier age. Self-reliance replaces the dole. Survival needs force painful changes. Struggle and suffering forge a new morality, stronger character and a rebirth of the rugged individualist. When the going gets tough the people rally. American exceptionalism overturns the naysayers.

In many ways the best thing that could happen to America is for the government to go broke. You won't find many people who share that view. In fact, you can hardly find anyone who thinks we are in serious enough trouble that the government can't fix it. Most people don't even think about such things. That's the way it was in Greece and Spain up to a few months ago.

CHAPTER FORTY-FIVE
$16,000,000,000,000

"Continued inflation inevitably leads to catastrophe."　　　　– Ludwig von Mises

"The devastation and the havoc that the runaway inflation causes among the populace is enormous. The relatively fixed-income groups are wiped out…society reverts to a state of virtual barter and complete impoverishment."

– Murray Rothbard

Nobody in America seems all that worried about $16 trillion in debt. But you should be. It's the reason you need to have silver and gold. Just a little pop in interest rates could ruin us. A bond buying strike by foreigners could spark runaway inflation. A decline in foreign demand for dollars could sink our currency and destroy the bond market. We're sitting on a powder keg attached to a burning fuse.

A bad outcome is inevitable. No country can spend recklessly on expensive social welfare schemes and in the face of a gargantuan, unprecedented debt bubble keep on spending with a vengeance. No country can subsidize rich and poor until half its population is on the dole. No country can have the world's biggest military, fight expensive wars and stick its nose in every country's business while spending wildly on foreign aid. It's not going to work. The train is leaving the station. The U.S. has cooked its goose. The sorry outcome is inevitable. The only question is when?

This country has gone mad. Our finances are in a shambles yet we persist in spending far more than we have. We borrow half of the money needed to finance our extravagances. Our politicians, courts and bureaucrats continue to add costly and expensive programs to our budget. Our monetary authorities print up the money that we can't borrow. This excess, this profligacy, this waste and wantonness will ultimately plunge us into despair. The arrogance, the heedlessness, the pride and the sophistry will bring us bitter tears. We are going to be humbled.

This country is in the grip of a falsehood that has risen to dominate the culture; the belief that big government is our savior. Our economists and our educators promote a radical dogma. Our media spreads the phony Keynesian doctrine of easy money. Envy and blind social sympathy pave the way to intervention and inflating. Creeping socialism demands runaway spending and inflation to thrive. It succeeds at the expense of free markets and capitalism. The powers that be and their intellectual cohorts sneer at enterprise and suck the marrow from the bones of the productive. No expense can be spared to implement the agenda of the left.

We are at $16 trillion and counting on the road to perdition. The big-spending progressive agenda is the blueprint for national ruin. Someday soon the bond vigilantes will arrive. Our bankruptcy is cooked in the books. What's left unsaid is that this winding path of excess and extravagance that we are following is more than just a road to national insolvency. It is the certain path to the extinction of everything that has made America great. It will be the end of us.

CHAPTER FORTY-SIX
WIPE OUT

"One of the worst features of all the plans for sharing the wealth and equalizing or guaranteeing incomes is that they lose sight of the conditions and institutions that are necessary to create wealth and income in the first place."

– Henry Hazlitt

"Throughout history governments have been chronically short of revenue. The reason should be clear: unlike you and me, governments do not produce useful goods and services that they can sell on the market; governments, rather than producing and selling services, live parasitically off the market and off society."

– Murray Rothbard

A country that does what America does to its money must suffer a terrible fall. We are stuck in the greatest predicament in history. Nobody sees it in Washington or Wall Street and the media is oblivious. A great crisis is upon us and we are reacting to it as we did with past problems, print up more money and hope the crisis goes away. This time it won't go away because our economic sins are too great.

Nothing other than capitalism creates prosperity on earth but we are replacing it with government initiatives that assure failure. The Feds control our money and in my opinion they are well on their way to ruining it. If any of us could truly comprehend the extent of our debt and our massive financial liabilities that person would quake with fear. The monetary authorities see no way out but to continue to do horrible things to our money. It's so serious that the repercussions will destroy all paper wealth. Those who listen to the politicians and the money managers will be ruined. Only tangible assets will survive.

At some point it will dawn on the populace that prices are going to keep rising because the central bank and the Treasury are going to persist in creating new money. More and more people will decide to spend the money rather than hold it because they know they can get goods cheaper today than they can tomorrow. Suddenly there's a rush to buy things.

Runaway inflation hits hard and fast. Prices explode. From $5.00 gasoline on Sunday to $10 on Monday and $25 on Tuesday. That's when most people become fearful. But for them it's too late. Because on Wednesday gas is $100 a gallon and a loaf of bread, $75.00. It gets worse, gas goes to $500 a gallon and the next day add a zero. In effect, the dollar has lost all its purchasing power in ten days. A million dollars in savings that once provided a financial cushion buys nothing.

Annuities, savings, money markets and bonds have quite suddenly lost all value. Along with the dollar they are worthless. The government's social security checks and other payments effectively bounce. They buy nothing. Washington's politicians and the Treasury announce a new currency. However, it's too late for the millions of savers and investors who relied on government to fix the economy. They lost everything.

You may think all of this sounds farfetched. From my perspective I think it's inevitable. Years ago much smarter economists than me wrote about the certainty of such an event. We are going to face national bankruptcy. We brought it on ourselves by embracing ruinous policies. We let liberalism run wild. The sorry outcome is now inevitable. Hope for the best but prepare for the worst.